Asian-
American
Women
Writers

Asian-American Women Writers

Edited and with an Introduction by

Harold Bloom

CHELSEA HOUSE PUBLISHERS
Philadelphia

ON THE COVER: *Topaz*, 1996, silkscreen, 22″ x 30″ by Tomie Arai.

CHELSEA HOUSE PUBLISHERS

EDITORIAL DIRECTOR Richard Rennert
PRODUCTION MANAGER Pamela Loos
PICTURE EDITOR Judy Hasday
ART DIRECTOR Sara Davis
SENIOR PRODUCTION EDITOR Lisa Chippendale

WOMEN WRITERS OF ENGLISH AND THEIR WORKS:
  Asian-American Women Writers

SERIES EDITOR Jane Shumate
CONTRIBUTING EDITOR Henna Remstein
ASSOCIATE EDITOR Therese De Angelis
INTERIOR AND COVER DESIGNER Alison Burnside
EDITORIAL ASSISTANT Anne Merlino

Introduction © 1997 by Harold Bloom

3 5 7 9 8 6 4 2

Library of Congress Cataloging-in-Publication Data

Asian American women writers / edited and with an introduction by
  Harold Bloom.
       p.   cm. — (Women writers of English and their works)
    Includes bibliographical references
    ISBN 0-7910-4475-0 (hc). — ISBN 0-7910-4491-2 (pbk.)
     1. American literature—Asian American authors—History and
  criticism. 2. American literature—Asian American authors—Bio
  –bibliography. 3. American literature—Women authors—History and
  criticism. 4. American literature—Women authors—Bio–bibliography.
  5. Asian Americans in literature. 6. Women and literature—United States.
  I. Bloom, Harold. II. Series.
  PS153.A84A83 1997
  810.9' 895' 0082—dc21

                                                                            97-9166
                                                                            CIP

Contents

Wakako Yamauchi 133

HAROLD BLOOM

I APPROACH THIS SERIES with a certain wariness, since so much of classical feminist literary criticism has founded itself upon arguments with that phase of my own work that began with *The Anxiety of Influence* (first published in January 1973). Someone who has been raised to that bad eminence—*The Patriarchal Critic*—is well advised that he trespasses upon sacred ground when he ventures to inquire whether indeed there are indisputable differences, imaginative and cognitive, between the literary works of women and those of men. If these differences are so substantial as pragmatically to make an authentic difference, does that in turn make necessary different aesthetic standards for judging the achievements of men and of women writers? Is Emily Dickinson to be read as though she has more in common with Elizabeth Barrett Browning than with Ralph Waldo Emerson?

Is Elizabeth Bishop a great poet because she triumphantly meets the same aesthetic criteria satisfied by Wallace Stevens, or should we evaluate her by criteria she shares with Marianne Moore, but not with Stevens? Are there crucial gender-based differences in the representations of Esther Summerson by Charles Dickens in *Bleak House*, and of Dorothea Brooke by George Eliot in *Middlemarch*? Does Samuel Richardson's Clarissa Harlowe convince us that her author was a male when we contrast her with Jane Austen's Elizabeth Bennet? Do women poets have a less agonistic relationship to female precursors than male poets have to their forerunners? Two eminent pioneers of feminist criticism, Sandra Gilbert and Susan Gubar, have suggested that women writers suffer more from an anxiety of authorship than they do from influence anxieties, while another important feminist critic, Elaine Showalter, has suggested that women writers, early and late, work together in a kind of quiltmaking, each doing her share while avoiding any contamination of creative envy in regard to other writers, provided that they be women. Can it be true that, in the aesthetic sphere, women do not beware women and do not suffer from the competitiveness and jealousy that alas do exist in the professional and sexual domains? Is there something in the area of literature, when practiced by women, that changes and purifies mere human nature?

I cannot answer any of these questions, yet I do think it is vital and clarifying to raise them. There is a current fashion, in many of our institutions of higher education, to insist that English Romantic poetry cannot be studied in the old way, with an exclusive emphasis upon the works of William Blake,

William Wordsworth, Samuel Taylor Coleridge, Lord Byron, Percy Bysshe Shelley, John Keats, and John Clare. Instead, the Romantic poets are taken to include Felicia Hemans, Laetitia Landon, Charlotte Smith, and Mary Tighe, among others. It would be heartening if we could believe that these are unjustly neglected poets, but their current revival will be brief. Similarly, anthologies of 17th-century English literature now tend to include the Duchess of Newcastle as well as Aphra Behn, Lady Mary Chudleigh, Anne Killigrew, Anne Finch, Countess of Winchilsea, and others. Some of these— Anne Finch in particular—wrote well, but a situation in which they are more read and studied than John Milton is not one that is likely to endure forever. The consequences of making gender a criterion for aesthetic choice must finally destroy all serious study of imaginative literature as such.

In their *Norton Anthology of Literature by Women,* Sandra Gilbert and Susan Gubar conclude their introduction to Elizabeth Barrett Browning by saying that "she constantly tested herself against the highest standards of male-defined poetic genres," a true if ambiguous observation. They then print her famous "The Cry of the Children," an admirably passionate ode that protests the cruel employment of little children in British Victorian mines and factories. Unfortunately, this well-meant prophetic affirmation ends with this, doubtless its finest stanza:

XIII
They look up with their pale and sunken faces,
    And their look is dread to see,
For they mind you of their angels in high places,
    With eyes turned on Deity.
"How long," they say, "how long, O cruel nation,
    Will you stand, to move the world, on a child's heart,—
Stifle down with a mailèd heel its palpitation,
    And tread onward to your throne amid the mart?
Our blood splashes upward, O goldheaper,
    And your purple shows your path!
But the child's sob in the silence curses deeper
    Than the strong man in his wrath."

If you read this aloud, then you may find yourself uncomfortable, on a strictly aesthetic basis, which would not vary if you were told that this had been composed by a male Victorian poet. In their selections from Elizabeth Bishop, Gilbert and Gubar courageously reprint Bishop's superb statement explaining her refusal to permit her poems to be included in anthologies of women's writing:

> Undoubtedly gender does play an important part in the making of any art, but art is art and to separate writings, paintings, musical compositions, etc., into sexes is to emphasize values in them that are *not* art.

That credo of Elizabeth Bishop's is to me the Alpha and Omega of critical wisdom in regard to all feminist literary criticism. Gender studies are precisely that: they study gender, and not aesthetic value. If your priorities are historical, social, political, and ideological, then gender studies clearly are more than justified. Perhaps they are a way to justice, or at least to more justice than women have received throughout thousands of years of male domination and aggression. Yet that is a very different matter from the now vexed issue of aesthetic value. Biographical criticism, like the different modes of historicist and psychological criticism, always has relied upon a kind of implicit gender studies and doubtless will benefit, as other modes will, by a making explicit of such considerations, particularly in regard to women writers.

Each volume in this series contains copious refutations of, and replies to, the traditionally aesthetic stance that I have advocated here. These introductory remarks aspire only to a questioning, and not a challenging, of feminist literary criticism. There are no longer any Patriarchal Critics; they are all dinosaurs, fabulous beasts fit for revival only in horror films. Sometimes I sadly think of myself as Bloom Brontosaurus, amiably left behind by the fire and the flood. But more often I go on reading the great women writers, searching for the aesthetic difference that yet may prove to be there, but which has not yet been found.

I N T R O D U C T I O N

BY GENERAL CONSENT, the most influential narratives in Chinese-American literature to date are Maxine Hong Kingston's *The Woman Warrior* (1976) and Amy Tan's *The Joy Luck Club* (1989). I want to contrast Hong Kingston's "No Name Woman" to Tan's "Two Kinds," each excerpted from the now famous fictive autobiographies.

One of my growing convictions, founded upon the last 20 or so of my more than 40 years of teaching at Yale University, is that the life of the mind and the spirit in the United States will be dominated by Asian Americans in the opening decades of the 21st century. The intellectuals—the women and men of literature and the other arts, of science and scholarship, and of the learned professions—are emerging from the various Asian-American peoples. In this displacement, the roles once played in American culture and society by the children of Jewish immigrants to the United States are passing to the children of Asian immigrants, and a new phase of American literature will be one of the consequences. *The Woman Warrior* and *The Joy Luck Club* are likely someday to be seen as transitional works, early instances of something much stronger to which nevertheless they have contributed.

"No Name Woman" is Kingston's horrifying account of a doomed aunt, necessarily unknown to her niece, since her memory emerges only from one of the stories told by Kingston's mother. A ghastly, poignant figure from the family's Chinese past, the aunt drowned herself and her baby in a well because of the terrible persecution visited upon her family and herself by the other villagers when they realized she was about to bear an illegitimate child. After the villagers wreck the family's house and crops, the wretched aunt is repudiated by her relatives and told that she herself is an unborn ghost. Devastated by the rejection, the No Name Woman kills both the baby and herself. Kingston, her aunt's only memorialist, renders an ambiguous and powerful summation that is neither elegy nor tribute:

> In the twenty years since I heard this story I have not asked for
> details nor said my aunt's name; I do not know it. People who can
> comfort the dead can also chase after them to hurt them further—
> a reverse ancestor worship. The real punishment was not the raid
> swiftly inflicted by the villagers, but the family's deliberately forget-
> ting her. Her betrayal so maddened them, they saw to it that she
> would suffer forever, even after death. Always hungry, always need-
> ing, she would have to beg food from other ghosts, snatch and steal
> it from those whose living descendants give them gifts. She would
> have to fight the ghosts massed at crossroads for the buns a few
> thoughtful citizens leave to decoy her away from village and home so

that the ancestral spirits could feast unharassed. At peace, they could act like gods, not ghosts, their descent lines providing them with paper suits and dresses, spirit money, paper houses, paper automobiles, chicken, meat, and rice into eternity—essences delivered up in smoke and flames, steam and incense rising from each rice bowl. In an attempt to make the Chinese care for people outside the family, Chairman Mao encourages us now to give our paper replicas to the spirits of outstanding soldiers and workers, no matter whose ancestors they may be. My aunt remains forever hungry. Goods are not evenly distributed among the dead.

My aunt haunts me—her ghost drawn to me because now, after fifty years of neglect, I alone devote pages of paper to her, though not origamied into houses and clothes. I do not think she always means me well. I am telling on her, and she was a spite suicide, drowning herself in the drinking water. The Chinese are always very frightened of the drowned one, whose weeping ghost, wet hair hanging and skin bloated, waits silently by the water to pull down a substitute.

Is this also an instance of "reverse ancestor worship"? Clearly not, since Kingston both pities and fears her aunt's memory, or ghost: "My aunt remains always hungry." Beyond the fanciful play with superstition, the passage's resonance depends upon its ambivalent response to a village culture where adultery was an extravagance and so, in bad years, a crime. Kingston's ghosts find their literary effectiveness in their narrator's ambivalence, which is fascinated, yet also appalled, by the ancestral world of violence, paternalism, and repressed individuality.

Tan's "Two Kinds," in contrast, centers entirely upon a Chinese-American mother-daughter relationship, dominated by the mother's possessive love and ambition for her child, who rebels against the mother's expectations of a musical genius that the child simply does not have:

She yanked me by the arm, pulled me off the floor, snapped off the TV. She was frighteningly strong, half pulling, half carrying me toward the piano as I kicked the throw rugs under my feet. She lifted me up and onto the hard bench. I was sobbing by now, looking at her bitterly. Her chest was heaving even more and her mouth was open, smiling crazily as if she were pleased I was crying.

"You want me to be someone I'm not!" I sobbed. "I'll never be the kind of daughter you want me to be!"

"Only two kinds of daughters," she shouted in Chinese. "Those who are obedient and those who follow their own mind! Only one kind of daughter can live in this house. Obedient daughter!"

"Then I wish I wasn't your daughter. I wish you weren't my mother," I shouted. As I said these things I got scared. I felt like worms and toads and slimy things were crawling out of my chest, but it also felt good, as if this awful side of me had surfaced, at last.

"Too late change this," said my mother shrilly.

And I could sense her anger rising to its breaking point. I wanted to see it spill over. And that's when I remembered the babies she had lost in China, the ones we never talked about. "Then I wish I'd never been born!" I shouted. "I wish I were dead! Like them."

It was if I had said the magic words, Alakazam!—and her face went blank, her mouth closed, her arms went slack, and she backed out of the room, stunned, as if she were blowing away like a small brown leaf, thin, brittle, lifeless.

It is a different order of writing from Kingston's, the style demotic rather than high, and the storytelling art unhaunted by village mythologies. Yet in a lower key it affords something of Kingston's ambivalent study of the nostalgias for a lost world. The dead babies transform the mother's movement into a ghostly image of "blowing away like a small brown leaf, thin, brittle, lifeless." That image allies Tan to the more elaborate art of storytelling that Kingston also quarries ultimately out of the Chinese-American mother-daughter relationship.

Diana Chang

b. 1934

DIANA CHANG was born in 1934 in New York City to a Eurasian mother and Chinese father. She spent her early childhood in Beijing and Shanghai, however, until her family fled Communist China and returned to New York, where Chang's father began work as an architect. In New York, Chang attended high school and Barnard College, where she studied creative writing and read, among others, existentialist philosophers; she has said that she was especially affected by Kierkegaard. After graduating, she worked full time as a junior editor at various publishing houses but finally quit, despite economic difficulties, so that she could spend more time writing.

Her first novel, *The Frontiers of Love*, was published in 1956 to much critical acclaim. Five other novels and three collections of poetry followed. Pursuing "universal" themes, Chang has said that she often subsumes aspects of her Eurasian background "in the interests of other truths and recognitions"; one of her abiding preoccupations has been the issue of identity. Her work has also appeared in magazines, including *American Scholar, Nation, New Letters, New York Quarterly*, and *Virginia Quarterly Review*. She is an accomplished painter as well and has exhibited her work in solo and group shows.

Chang has taught creative writing and interdisciplinary art courses at Barnard College and currently lives in Water Mill, New York.

CRITICAL EXTRACTS

SAMANTHA RAMA RAU

The pathos and the problems of the Eurasian in Asia have, for a long time, interested Westerners, sometimes from the point of view of the Eurasians' anomalous political position, and sometimes (notably in the writing of Joseph Hitrec and John Masters) because of their emotional complexities. It is relatively seldom, however, that one is given a convincing and interior view of the Eurasian world, written, so to speak, from the inside looking out and embracing both the political and emotional dilemmas of that twilit no-man's-land.

Whether or not Diana Chang's "The Frontiers of Love" is largely autobiographical is a matter of complete irrelevance, for she brings to the background and descriptive detail of her story an authenticity that stands up equally well as fact or fiction. She has chosen for the setting of her novel a bleak period in the history of China in general and of Shanghai in particular—the stagnant, demoralized life of the last weeks of the Japanese Occupation, and the chaotic months following.

Her chief characters are all Eurasians or Chinese and foreigners inextricably entangled in the Eurasian situation. ⟨. . .⟩

Within their narrow orbit all of them try to work out their own destinies and convictions and satisfactions. ⟨. . .⟩

Meanwhile some of the "neutrals," some of the other Eurasians, some of the foreigners married to Chinese, dream of escape, identity, security in America, in Europe, anywhere except Shanghai.

If Miss Chang's sense of characterization—intense and painfully honest as it often is—needs some extra authority and experience, the reader is amply compensated in her fine sense of a city's atmosphere and moods, in a lovely and moving description of a child's view of Peiping, in her feeling for that tragically ineffectual figure—the creature destined for betrayal—the Chinese liberal.

—Samantha Rama Rau, "The Need to Belong," *The New York Times Book Review* (23 September 1956): 4, 26

KENNETH REXROTH

Diana Chang has written of a miniature society entrapped and suspended, a social Mohammed's coffin, a space platform lost beyond the moon. Yet, of all the novels of the Far East published this season, her book, at least for me, has most reality. Partly it is because her people are more like you and me, more typically part of the world-wide community of a sick Western society than Japanese fishermen or wastrel poets, and so more accessible; partly it is because Chinese civilization, which after all is still their strong foundation, is, in spite of all its current vicissitudes, a deeper and richer thing than Japanese; partly it is a matter of style. Miss Chang's style may not be faultless, but it is certainly personal, and it is more alive, more gripping, than even the best translation. Then, too, all the world can be reflected in a mirror on a space station, however lost, and so she has managed to embody much, if not all, of the forces acting on human beings caught in the maelstrom of total transvaluation which is the twentieth-century Far East. Like the situation, her characters are dramatically "pure," almost like Ben Jonson's humors—imperialists; international gadabouts; aging liberal Chinese incapable of decision; a youth from the countryside, spontaneously, organically revolutionary, who is crushed by the blind melodrama of organized "revolution"; and the women, all of them seeking love, all of them losing it, and one of them, a rather autobiographical-sounding heroine, at least finding a kind of personal integrity in tragedy and betrayal. Once again, it is the same message as in so many of these novels, "Out of this nettle, alienation, we pluck this flower, integrity." Not very many first novels are written with as much skill and insight.

—Kenneth Rexroth, "World Ills in the Far East," *The Nation* (29 September 1956): 272

JANICE BISHOP

What Matisse Is After is poetry with an economy of language as elegantly inclusive as the line and motion rendered by the French master himself. To read these poems exploring paradoxical perception is to breathe in the rhythmic interplay of word, image, idea, feeling. Each synthesizes one into the other, simulating change which, like the lines of Matisse, are a *departure / toward returning / in the teeth of our dying*.

Natural, human, and aesthetic experience are mutually transposed in "As Green Comes." Generated by breath/spirit the appearance of poems is analogous to both the pubescent breasts of girls and nature's budding. Significantly, in "A Double Pursuit," the painter signs not the perishable canvas but ephemeral air, the spirit's mode. Light/energy are synecdochic of spirit infusing meaning. Many poems emit a phosphorescent glow. In "Wonder" personified light reflects itself enabling us to see objects. Through light a person becomes *extraordinary*. ⟨. . .⟩

Although Diana Chang uses ethnic referents, she moves outside the boundaries of ethnicity. In "On Gibson Lane, Sagaponack" she speaks of her Chinese strangeness in an Anglo culture. Yet, she and a blond girl share the experience of riding *along the same edge* of being; each mysteriously evolving, then returning to self.

In "Twelve-Year-Olds," the room which is a *tunnel* is given motion by the dance of blossoming pre-adolescents. As mantises, they are both prophets and insects groping with *tuxedo-elegance*, as if *praying* against a backdrop of *centuries of jungles*.

What Matisse Is After opens and closes in perfect symmetry. A surge of green transposing into growing bodies of girls, like Matisse's women effortlessly filling space, returns as nature's disordered dance. Energy languorously evolving, convoluting the animistic and human, instinctively flourishes.

—Janice Bishop, [Review of *What Matisse Is After*], *The Forbidden Stitch: An Asian American Women's Anthology*, ed. Shirley Lim and Mayumi Tsutakawa (Corvallis, OR: Calyx Books, 1989), 242–43

AMY LING

In *Frontiers of Love*, Chang makes clear that one's identity is the sum of all of one's past, not the choice of one half of one's ancestry at the expense of the other, the mistake made by Feng Huang and Mimi Lambert. For Sylvia Chen and for Diana Chang, this past includes nostalgic memories of early childhood in Peiping (Beijing) 〈. . .〉 How different is Diana Chang's sun—"the boldness, the lustiness, the fullblown wonder of solid sunlight"—from Eileen Chang's (no relation) exhausted sun—lying "across the street like an old yellow dog, barring the way"—in *The Rice Sprout Song*. In this passage, Diana Chang strongly affirms the centrality of her own past. The depth of feeling for these childhood memories of her natal city goes beyond fondness or affection; it is an attachment like an umbilical cord: the central and essential sustenance necessary to the life of every adult. Chang makes no apologies but simply and boldly states that *everyone's* "first memories . . . should be under the Peiping sky." This proud assertion counteracts the painfully alienated description of Peiyuan's Chinese ugliness. Taken together, the two passages express the double consciousness of what it means to be Chinese in a white world. 〈. . .〉

The golden memory of Peiping is but the foundation for building a cosmopolitanism and expatriation "free from any narrow chauvinism." Indeed, for Diana Chang "to be Chinese was not enough," for her five later novels, with a single minor exception, do not have Chinese or Amerasian characters in them at all. Asked why her later protagonists were all Caucasian, she replied that "exoticism" can stand in the way of the "universal" she strives for in her themes and, therefore, she has "often subsumed aspects of her background in the interest of other truths." Asked why a Chinese or Chinese American can't also be "universal," she responded that we are living in the United States and "Everyman" here is white. Though an ethnic minority writer is not bound to write of her own ethnicity, as women writers are not bound to create only heroines nor to adopt a feminist perspective, nonetheless, prolonged avoidance of that which is closest to one's self when self-hood is one's major theme is a difficult stand to defend. The explanation may be that Diana Chang's formative years were spent in the United States, in New York City, during the McCarthy era, when all Americans, including Chinese Americans, had to disavow everything having to do with a Communist country, and China, of course, was Communist. Thus, the central characters of five of her six novels are white Anglo-Saxon Protestants with the occasional "exotic," a Jew. In her poetry and recent short fiction, however, Chang has treated Chinese American subjects.

—Amy Ling, *Between Worlds: Women Writers of Chinese Ancestry* (Elmsford, NY: Pergamon Press, 1990), 118–19

AMY LING

Writing is an act of self-assertion, self-revelation, and self-preservation. One writes out of a delight in one's storytelling powers, out of a need to reveal and explain oneself, or from a desire to record and preserve experience. However, for women brought up in the old Chinese tradition that for eighteen hundred years codified their obedience and submission to the men in their lives— father, husband, son—a tradition that stressed female chastity, modesty, and restraint; that broke girls' toes and bound their feet as an ideal of beauty; that sold daughters into slavery in times of hardship; that encouraged and honored widow suicides—any writing at all was unusual, even an act of rebellion. ⟨. . .⟩ Furthermore, since it was the Chinese custom to leave the women at home when the men first immigrated, temporarily they thought, to the Gold Mountain to make their fortunes, the number of Chinese women in America was small. In 1852, for example, of the 11,794 Chinese in California, only 7 were women, and most of these were prostitutes. ⟨. . . The⟩ numbers of Chinese women in the United States did not approach equality with Chinese men until 1954. Thus it is not surprising that we have so little writing by Chinese American women; it is notable that we have so much. ⟨. . .⟩

⟨. . . The⟩ majority of Chinese American works are by immigrants and sojourners, daughters of diplomats and scholars, and those who have had contact with the West through missionaries or mission schools. For the immigrant, the very act of choosing to write in English, a second language, and thereby addressing a predominantly Caucasian audience is significant and colors the purpose and nature of the work. ⟨. . . I⟩mmigrant and sojourner Chinese American writers ⟨. . .⟩ seek primarily to explain and justify China and Chinese ways to the Western world. ⟨. . .⟩ Transplanted after their formative years, they see their role in the West as interpreters and ambassadors of good will and understanding for China; to borrow David Riesman's term, they are "other-directed."

American-born Chinese American writers, ⟨. . .⟩ however, tend to be more individualistic and to have an inward focus. Because they have grown up as a racial minority, imbibing the customs of two cultures, their centers are not stable and single. Their consciousness, as W. E. B. Du Bois pointed out for African Americans, is double; their vision bifocal and fluctuating. Therefore, they look inward with an urgency to comprehend and balance the bicultural clashes they have known and must reconcile. That they write and publish is of course indicative of an awareness of an external world and a desire to communicate, but their initial impetus is primarily introspective. Their purpose is to explain themselves to themselves. ⟨. . .⟩

With two exceptions, Diana Chang's books have nothing to do with Chinese or Chinese Americans. Her first work, *Frontiers of Love*, a rich, full novel set in Shanghai at the close of World War II, is the story of three young Eurasians, representing the spectrum of possibilities in the struggle to determine their identities. ⟨. . .⟩ Chang, who is three-quarters Chinese and one-quarter Irish but by upbringing an American, ⟨like her character Sylvia Chen⟩ acts for herself instead of reacting and goes her own way in her other novels.

Chang chooses in her later books to focus on modern varieties of love: love after divorce, in *A Woman of Thirty*; love for an unborn child, even if it is the result of rape, in *A Passion for Life*; interracial love between a Caucasian Peace Corps volunteer and a Chinese Communist dancer, in the minor, farcical *The Only Game in Town*; love as a manifestation of neurosis, in the clever *Eye to Eye*, in which a married white Protestant artist falls in love with a Jewish writer and seeks the help of a psychiatrist; extramarital love between an older woman and a younger man, in *A Perfect Love*. She writes with great skill of Ivy League graduates, artists, writers, publishers, who inhabit the world of New York City, Long Island, Massachusetts. Her characters tend to be blue-eyed Anglo-Saxons; the outsiders are Jews. "Fitness, in evolutionary biology," says the biologist Lewis Thomas, "means fitting in with the rest of life. If a species is good at this, it tends to survive" (32). Like Winnifred Eaton, Diana Chang is conscious of her audience and wants to fit in, to survive; she "subsumes aspects of her background in the interests of other truths" (qtd. in Ling, "Writer" 75), truths she believes will have a broader appeal in the society in which she lives.

—Amy Ling, "Chinese American Women Writers: The Tradition behind Maxine Hong Kingston," *Redefining American Literary History*, ed. A. LaVonne Brown Ruoff and Jerry W. Ward, Jr. (New York: The Modern Language Association of America, 1990), 219–20, 233

SHIRLEY GEOK-LIN LIM

The theme of being in the world can be seen not solely as a search for identity but as a quest for selfness. It is a theme that has resonated in American literature from the opening line in *Moby-Dick*, "Call me Ishmael," to Ralph Ellison's "I am the invisible man." To a writer such as Diana Chang, plot and characterization, no longer mere devices to explore ethnicity or to protest political trauma, become the means by which characters' selves evolve or are examined. In Chang's novels, the questions of stereotypes, ethnicity, duality, and the forging of a new identity fall under a larger existentialist theme. In most of the works of the Asian American writers discussed so far, authorial identity is indistinguishable from the author's ethnic identity; but Chang is a protean author, a master of disguises whose authorial identity cannot be fixed by ethnicity. In *Eye to Eye*, her fifth novel, for example, the narrator and main character is a white Anglo-Saxon American male married to a long-legged blonde and infatuated with a Jewish woman. What frees Chang to explore the broader oceans of consciousness is her ability to construct alternative points of view. Obviously influenced by Ford Madox Ford, her secular, urban fictions express an intense consciousness of self through this manipulation.

Her first novel, *The Frontiers of Love*, shows her early, abiding attachment to a form of controlling mask and masking control. Begun as an inchoate personal narrative, it was reworked into fiction through the creation of five characters caught in the inertia and anarchy of wartime Shanghai. Through their points of view, Chang examines the inadequacy of racial identity in providing us with a sense of self. Through the tragedies of two young Eurasians, Mimi and Feng Huang, we learn that the alienated and unreflecting self, in its desperation to escape the terrors of freedom (that is, absence of racial belonging), destroys itself. Sylvia, the third Eurasian, alone knows that "if one did not hold on carefully to one's sense of self, one might wake up some morning looking for one's face, so easily lost" (87). Sylvia escapes self-destruction, for in her absence of narrow commitment to race is her capacity for insight. Aware of her dual racial origins, she is unwilling to sacrifice one for the other; aware of the individual's vulnerability in search of self-definition, she is capable of objectivity. Her search for point of view is finally more authentic than "a single comforting bias" (18). The novel ends with Liyi's, Sylvia's father's, vision that "life was not to be resolved, but to be lived—a constant improvisation" (245). The spontaneous creation of self in its encounters with the world, a brave existentialist answer to the question of identity, is Chang's special contribution to Asian American literature.

According to Irving Howe, "what usually shapes a new literary movement is less a common future than a common rejection of the recently dominant past." It is clear in Asian American writing that those literary works that most exploit the dominant stereotypes of their racial history are less powerfully works of imagination. When Asian American writers reject the "recently dominant past," choosing instead, like Kingston and Chang, to construct the fiction of a memory that never took place, their work becomes empowered with the consciousness of literary text.

—Shirley Geok-lin Lim, "Twelve Asian American Writers: In Search of Self-Definition," *Redefining American Literary History*, ed. A. LaVonne Brown Ruoff and Jerry W. Ward, Jr. (New York: The Modern Language Association of America, 1990), 249

L. M. GROW

In "Four Views of Reality," published in *The American Scholar* 25:1 (1955–56): 67–68, Diana Chang treats, respectively, painting, music, and poetry in the first three poems and illustrates the applications of all three in the fourth poem. Each of these arts is a means of escape from the Euclidean world of restriction, where "the circling of infinity" incarcerates the human spirit: "Nowhere in Manhattan does Euclid cease. / Music sings drily into toneless equations."

Paradoxically, imagination creates freedom not from vast vistas but in "imagination's small society," whether the dimension is horizontal ("New England's blue geography"), as in the first poem, or vertical, as in the second ("Music is prismatic among these heights, / [in Manhattan] . . . dumb warm circuits dominate / A low, miraculous firmament of air"). In the case of "hosannas to truth," the "human position" (metaphysical posture?, existential predicament?) is a "fiction" if it is measured in longitude and latitude. If one wishes to map essence, the "dumb warm circuits" of the hosannas to truth, not the circles of infinity, must be used for the purpose. ⟨. . .⟩

"Four Views in Praise of Reality" is a subtle, finely-wrought, thoughtful set of poems, and that judgment can be tested by the stanzaic structure as well as by a close examination of the content. The first poem's stanzas are, respectively, a quatrain and two tercets. Poems two and four consist entirely of tercets, and poem number three exclusively of quatrains. The balance of quatrain to tercet found in poem number one has a mirror image in the succeeding three verses, containing as they do collectively six tercets and three quatrains. This two-to-one ratio is inversely present in the two quatrains and one tercet of poem number one. To extend this numerical count one step further, we might note one of the most readily apparent features of this quartet: there are *four* poems, each of which contains *three* stanzas. Threes and fours are juxtaposed meaningfully but not mechanically, so that we have a temptation to interpret the numerical significance but no clear-cut answers after we have done so. Do we have four views (and quatrain construction in parts) because the classical division of the earth's elements was into four parts? Do tercets abound because three has from antiquity been a number symbolic of a perfect, finished state? Is there a useful conclusion to be derived from the intermixing of an even (four) and an odd (three) number? Does their arithmetical total of seven, with that number's long history of connotations, have a design behind it? The richness and subtlety of response possible is itself Diana Chang's escape from the Euclidean world of restriction—and this escape becomes, after we have carefully read "Four Views in Praise of Reality" our escape as well.

—L. M. Grow, "On Diana Chang's 'Four Views in Praise of Reality,'" *Amerasia Journal* 16, no. 1 (1990): 211, 214–15

SAU-LING CYNTHIA WONG

Diana Chang's 1989 short story, "The Oriental Contingent," provides ancillary evidence that culture is a relatively insignificant factor in Asian American versions of the double. This story explores the ambivalence of American-born Chinese who feel *inferior* for being assimilated. Connie Sung, a third-generation pianist, meets a Chinese American woman with the name of Lisa Mallory, which Connie assumes comes from marrying a Caucasian. For three or four years after their first meeting, Connie is plagued by bewilderment at Lisa's aloofness. Considering herself a "failed Chinese" (174), Connie concludes that Lisa must be "Chinese-Chinese" (173); the latter's reticence must be a matter of tact, to protect the feelings of the less fortunate.

Finally, at a chance encounter, Lisa confesses to Connie that she was born in Buffalo and adopted by white parents. The two women have in fact been feeling defensive toward each other, each believing the other to be more Chinese, each trying to hide her own lack of cultural authenticity. They have been each other's ethnic "secret sharer," so to speak. Lisa exclaims: "The only time I feel Chinese is when I'm embarrassed I'm not more Chinese—which is a totally Chinese reflex that I'd give anything to be rid of!" Connie knows that "none of this matters to anybody except us" but cannot help feeling cursed.

> "It's only Orientals who haunt me!" Lisa stamped her foot. "Only them!"
> "I'm so sorry," Connie Sung said, for all of them.
> "It's all so turned around." (177)

While Chang's short story is so sketchy that all our inferences must be tentative, the sense of tension, fascination, and haunting that the two characters feel toward each other suggests a possible reading of the story as one of the double, with this critical difference: that everything about the two main characters is "turned around," a mirror image of the situation in ⟨Maxine Hong Kingston's⟩ *The Woman Warrior* or ⟨Monica Sone's⟩ *Nisei Daughter*. Connie and Lisa feel stigmatized and diminished for being too Americanized. They have internalized the disdain that "Chinese-Chinese" hold for the American-born. Each woman projects onto the other all the strengths that she wishes she had: direct access to the Chinese community, familiarity with Chinese culture, self-assurance, security of identity. The "Asian" side of the self, not the "American," is the favored one.

Now if cultural conflict could adequately account for the phenomenon of the racial shadow, we would expect to see more stories like "The Oriental Contingent," for then both the "Asian" and the "American" aspects of the self would have an equal chance to be repressed and projected. What we find instead is that the theoretical possibility hinted at in "The Oriental Contingent" is hardly ever actualized in Asian American literature, for the simple reason that the prevailing asymmetry in interracial relationships makes such actualization unlikely. For Asian Americans, incomplete assimilation to white standards is more liable to create embarrassment or insecurity than lapses from Asian standards, which are not taken into account by those who dominate the power structure of the country.

—Sau-ling Cynthia Wong, *Reading Asian American Literature: From Necessity to Extravagance* (Princeton: Princeton University Press, 1993), 98–99

Shirley Geok-lin Lim

The Frontiers of Love was first published in 1956 to much acclaim. But nowhere was it hailed then as an Asian American work. The republication of Diana Chang's formidable first novel by the University of Washington Press is a belated recognition that the novel is one of the earliest transgressors of canonical frontiers. It queried categories of identity—national, racial, class, and gender—at a time when American readers in the main were not merely unmindful of issues of diversity but when powerful state forces were inimical to any suggestions of deviance from the jingoistic and hysterical brand of patriotism that Joseph McCarthy had hijacked as his terrain. ⟨. . .⟩

Set in 1945, *The Frontiers of Love* was already in some ways a historical novel when it appeared in 1956. The experiences it represented, of the Second World War's exiled and interned characters in Japanese-occupied Shanghai, are even further removed for the generation of readers in the last decade of the twentieth century. Thus, in crucial ways, the novel must be read in its historical context. The dilatory yet tense, superficially pleasure-loving yet paranoid intensity of the novel's social world suggests the tenor of relations in a specific cosmopolitan milieu in response to eight years of militaristic rule. The novel constructs the sensibility of a particular society undergoing a crisis of an interregnum: the characters are isolated individuals thrown together by the political violence of war into an inescapable community of transients, exiles, aliens, and sojourners, each seeking solace and satisfaction in the constrained space of a hostile occupied territory. ⟨. . .⟩

⟨The⟩ Westernized milieu of Shanghai dominates *The Frontiers of Love*. As Sylvia Chen notes in the novel, "The Shanghai which she knew was circumscribed, uncontaminated by the Chinese section, which she had never even visited" (p. 85). Yet in the novel's self-conscious gaps, its self-reflexive interrogations of its own settings, lies a strict condemnation of Western colonialism and its cultural consequences, the anomie, alienation, deracination, and psychopolitical depredations in the wake of Western imperialism. The Shanghai cosmopolites were "unnamed hybrids," "survivors of a colonialism that was fast becoming as antique as peace" (p. 86). Embedded in Chinese society, colonialist racism "held them apart (from the Chinese) in a trance" (p. 87).

Chang's fictive commentary on the problematic of the colonized is contemporary with Frantz Fanon's study of the colonized in *Black Skin, White Masks* (first published in Paris in 1952): "People were true to nothing in Shanghai; they belonged only to the surface values of both East and West and leaned heavily toward the exoticism of the West. If one did not hold on carefully to one's sense of self, one might wake up one morning looking for one's face, so easily lost" (p. 87). The sentence expresses both nostalgia for a truth, for those deeper values of a culture, whether East or West, that can provide an individual with a sense of unity and coherence, and a consciousness of its unavailability. "Face" here signifies not merely the physicality that functions as a marker of race and thus of cultural identity but more complexly the Chinese notion of self-respect within a society, that is, the specific social positions of individuals. The consciousness of a Chinese majority shut out of the foreground of dramatic action gives the novel its complicating thematics of race and culture.

Shanghai as a metaphor for a historical and political identity reminds us that the boundaries which we think of as defining national, cultural, racial, gender, and other identities are inherently unstable. As political and epistemological construction, Shanghai was both Chinese and Western, native and foreign, liberatory and oppressive, national and international. Like the three major youthful characters (Sylvia, Feng, and Mimi), it literalizes the identity "Eurasian": "Shanghai [was] a Eurasian city" (93). As Feng, the son of a neurasthenic Englishwoman and remote Chinese father, acknowledges, it is Shanghai's duplicity, its Western colonized culture, that contributes to his identity confusion: "Strictly speaking, it could not be called Chinese, though it was inhabited mostly by Chinese—Chinese who were either wealthy, Westernized or prayed to a Christian God" (p. 21). For Feng, questing for ego coherence and unity which he has conceptualized as single-race identity, such cultural doubleness, figured in the material culture of Shanghai, is intolerable.

Thus the novel is not simply a historical novel, although it offers pleasures even on that limited level. In its almost faultless structuring of multiple points of view it plays out obsessive interrogations and reinscriptions of identity that deconstruct the usual notions of national, racial, class, and gender identities into their phenomenological and epistemological brittleness. As policed borders or as cultural and racial expression, the novel represents Shanghai as the site of violent fragmenting identities, of conflicting evolving and contingent futures. The frontiers "of love" delineate the psychosexual and sociopolitical processes, the "imaginings" through which individuals and nations unmake and make themselves.

—Shirley Geok-lin Lim, "Introduction" to *The Frontiers of Love* by Diana Chang (Seattle: University of Washington Press, 1994), v–ix

LEO HAMALIAN

⟨**Diana Chang**:⟩ ⟨. . .⟩ At the time that *The Frontiers of Love* was published, most of the very favorable reviews seemed to take it simply as a novel, a literary effort. Can it be said that there was some merit in that? I believe so at least part of the time.

I wasn't pigeonholed by the mainstream press. In fact, misunderstood in ethnic circles that both adopted and disapproved of it, it was a novel some of them tried to force into an ideological Procrustes bed, regarding it as a novel about minority characters living in this country. I was quite baffled, truth to tell. *I* knew the book is set entirely in Shanghai, China, and while it is about identity, it is not about ethnicity here. I hope everyone will read Shirley Lim's introduction ⟨. . . .⟩

My Chinese characters are not particularly exotic, and one can wonder why. Is it because their middle-classness frees them from characteristics the average American reader looks for in Asians, traits that perhaps they find appealingly different from their own and foreign enough to escape the hum-drum, and therefore are picturesque? Everyone is eager for a change of scene, after all.

A contemporary Chinese physician, professor or lawyer in Hong Kong, Beijing or Taipei is not so different in his values, outlook and goals for himself and his children from his counterpart in New York City or Minneapolis. He is not necessarily deeply steeped only in his own traditional customs and mores, folklore, superstitions, and mindset. (They're reading Kurt Vonnegut in Taipei.) In other words, the cultural differences that readers here find intrigu-ing may be found not so much horizontally—across the Pacific Ocean—but in the verticality of social strata and its diversity.

My work is different for a second reason: while my novel *The Only Game in Town*, an East-West spoof, also draws on my Chinese-American background, my other four novels could have been written by anyone, say, a Diana Smith. It has perplexed and bothered me that this has breached, in some eyes, pro-scriptions I was unaware of at first.

As David Henry Hwang put it—and I remember what he said almost word for word: In this country today, only blacks can write about blacks, only women about women, only Asian Americans about Asian Americans, but white males can write about anyone.

An interesting observation from him, and he has many. I'm happy that David has written about the sexual ambivalence of a French diplomat in his remarkable play, *M. Butterfly*, now also a film, and that Kazuo Ishiguro, whose background is Japanese and who lives in London, explored in his brilliant novel, *The Remains of the Day*, the life, misapprehensions and inhibitions of an elderly English butler—*in the first person.*

Supposing they had restricted themselves to Asian American themes and characters . . . what a loss it would have been. We all live in the world, an increasingly global village. Why not write about others? Why should anyone disfranchise him or herself from any human history or experience? Is anything human alien?

—Leo Hamalian, "A *MELUS* Interview: Diana Chang," *MELUS* 20, no. 4 (Winter 1995): 39–40

BIBLIOGRAPHY

The Frontiers of Love. 1956.
A Woman of Thirty. 1959.
A Passion for Life. 1961.
The Only Game in Town. 1963.
Eye to Eye. 1974.
A Perfect Love. 1978.
The Horizon Is Definitely Speaking. 1982.
What Matisse Is After. 1984.
Earth Water Light. 1991.

Edith Maude Eaton

1865–1914

Winnifred Eaton

1875–1954

MOST SCHOLARS consider Edith Maude Eaton and Winnifred Eaton the first Chinese-American women writers. Their Chinese mother, Grace (Lotus Blossom) Trefusis, was educated in England by missionaries and then returned to China, where she met Edward Eaton, an English silk merchant. They married, eventually moved to Montreal, Canada, and had 14 children. Neither Edith nor Winnifred looked particularly Asian, but they grew up poor and regularly confronted class and racial discrimination—a subject both women would later explore in their writings. However, their paths to literary success took dramatically different courses.

Edith Eaton was born in England, but, because British society frowned upon her parents' interracial marriage, the family emigrated when she was six to Montreal, where, unhappily, tolerance was not much greater. The prejudice Edith experienced in both countries greatly influenced her writing career. She embraced and defended her heritage, writing mostly about Chinese- and Asian-American topics under the pen name Sui Sin Far (also Sui Sin Fah or Sui Seen Far). Articles and short stories published in several Montreal newspapers and magazines launched her career in Canada. After she moved to the United States in 1898, where she lived in various West Coast Chinatowns (principally in Seattle and San Francisco), her work began to appear in American magazines. She is perhaps best known for the autobiographical essay "Leaves from the Mental Portfolio of an Eurasian," which details the social alienation and suffering she experienced as a biracial woman. Edith Eaton never married and, at the age of 49, died of heart disease, soon after publishing her only book-length work, *Mrs. Spring Fragrance*.

Winnifred Eaton also left Canada as a young adult, first to Jamaica for a brief stint as a newspaper reporter, and then to Chicago, where she worked as a typist while completing her first novel, *Miss Numè of Japan*. Quite in contrast to her sister, Winnifred Eaton appropriated a Japanese persona and began using the Japanese-sounding pseudonym

Onoto Watanna—perhaps to distinguish herself from her sister, or possibly to play on America's sentimentality at the time toward the Japanese. In fact, period photographs show her wearing a kimono, hair piled atop her head in traditional Japanese style. Later, in New York City, she met and married Bertrand W. Babcock, with whom she had four children. The marriage was strained by his alcoholism, however, and they eventually divorced; she later returned to her native Canada with her second husband, Francis Fournier Reeve. With her various marriages and pseudonyms, the record of her life and work appears under many names; in addition to those mentioned, she is also known as Winnifred Eaton Reeve, Winnifred Babcock, and Winnifred Babcock Reeve.

Primarily writing formulaic romance novels that pair a Japanese or Eurasian woman with an English or American man, Winnifred Reeve paid such close attention to Japanese cultural and linguistic idiosyncrasies that she fooled fans and critics alike. She also wrote a novel with an Irish-American protagonist (written under the name Winnifred Mooney) and several regional books about cattle ranching set in Canada. Though they were relatively well received, she achieved her great popular and financial success publishing the best-selling melodramas with predictable, sentimental outcomes for their Japanese heroines. From 1925 to 1932, she wrote and edited film scripts in Hollywood, many of them adaptations of her own novels, but, regrettably, she was not credited in most of them. She died, likely of natural causes, on April 8, 1954.

C R I T I C A L   E X T R A C T S

THE NEW YORK TIMES REVIEW OF BOOKS

Miss ⟨Edith Maude⟩ Eaton has struck a new note in American fiction. She has not struck it very surely, or with surpassing skill. But it has taken courage to strike it at all, and, to some extent, she atones for lack of artistic skill with the unusual knowledge she undoubtedly has of her theme. The thing she has tried to do is to portray for readers of the white race the lives, feelings, sentiments of the Americanized Chinese of the Pacific Coast, or those who have intermarried with them and of the children who have sprung from such unions. It is a task whose adequate doing would require well-nigh superhuman insight and the subtlest of methods. In some of the stories she seems not even to have tried to see inside the souls of her people, but has contented herself with the merest sketching of externals. In others, again, she has seen far and deep, and has made her account keenly interesting. Especially is this true of the analysis she makes occasionally of the character of an Americanized Chinese, of the glimpses she gives into the lives, thoughts and emotions of the Chinese women who refuse to be anything but intensely Chinese, and into the characters of the half-breed children.

    —N.A., [Review of *Mrs. Spring Fragrance*], *The New York Times Review of Books* (7 July 1912): 405

AMY LING

⟨Edith Eaton's⟩ ethnicity was a painful, ever-present aspect of her life, and her sensitivity to others' curiosity and contempt was acute. Her autobiographical article, "Leaves from the Mental Portfolio of an Eurasian," published in the January 21, 1909, issue of the *Independent*, is a moving, gracefully written account of the painful experience of growing up Eurasian in prejudiced nineteenth-century England and America.

    Her first memory, of an event that occurred when she was scarcely four years old, was of walking down a green English lane in front of her nurse and overhearing the woman tell her friend that her charge's mother is Chinese: " 'Oh Lord!' exclaims the informed. She turns me around and scans me curiously from head to foot. Then the two women whisper together" (p. 125). Edith does not understand their consternation and curiosity, but she cannot help but realize that others perceive her as different, strange, and somehow inferior. As a six year old in Hudson City, New York, she and her brother are drawn into a fight with hostile children who mock the Chinese: "They pull my hair, they tear my clothes, they scratch my face, and all but lame my brother; but the white blood in our veins fights valiantly for the Chinese half of us" (p. 126). Repeated incidents of being hooted or stared at intensify her sensitivity, but she fortifies herself by positive action, going to the library and reading everything she can find about China and the Chinese, thereby developing pride in herself and her background. She later discovers, however, that her mother's people are just as narrow-minded as her father's and that many full-blooded Chinese have a prejudice against the half-white. She envisions a happier future ruled by love rather than blindness:

> Only when the whole world becomes as one family will human
> beings be able to see clearly and hear distinctly. I believe that some
> day a great part of the world will be Eurasian. I cheer myself with the
> thought that I am but a pioneer. A pioneer should glory in suffering.
> (p. 129) ⟨. . .⟩

Throughout her life, thereafter, Edith Eaton published short stories and articles concerning Chinese-American life 〈. . . .〉 In 1912, A. C. McClurg and Company of Chicago collected thirty-seven of these stories in a volume entitled after the first story, *Mrs. Spring Fragrance*. In a florid fashion, the vermillion cover is embossed in gold letters and decorated with lotus flowers, a dragonfly and the moon. The pages are gray-green, lightly imprinted with a Chinese-style painting of a crested bird on a branch of bamboo, a flowering branch of plum and the Chinese characters for Happiness, Prosperity, and Longevity vertically descending along the right side. Eaton's stories, some appropriately charming and lively, others, however, striking ironic, even bitter, notes, are printed on these delicately decorated sheets.

The best stories are the serious and tragic ones in which the characters are real and their problems moving; the least successful are those in which the reader feels the author's straining to present an image of the Chinese as charming, quaint, and lovable, and for which happy endings are contrived. The reviews were mostly favorable. 〈. . .〉

〈. . .〉 No one before her had written so sympathetically and so extensively about the Chinese in America, and never before from this far inside. In fictional form, she could express her sense of outrage through veiled sarcasm and ironic reversals; she could draw forth the reader's sympathy by presenting the emotions and daily lives of characters who were appealing and deeply human. Her themes are universal—love of men and women, parents and children, brothers and sisters, and the forces that thwart this love. Eaton expects readers to identify with the love-drive of her characters, and she hopes that readers will condemn the thwarting forces, even if these happen to be their own laws and practices. Her other themes are women's rights, especially those of the working women; the bond of friendship among women; idealism and cynicism; betrayal and retribution.

—Amy Ling, "Edith Eaton: Pioneer Chinamerican Writer and Feminist," *American Literary Realism, 1870–1910* 16, no. 2 (Autumn 1983): 288–89, 291–92

AMY LING

The Japanese persona 〈. . .〉 was undoubtedly the predominant one in the life and writing career of Winnifred Eaton. We can imagine the young Winnifred, setting out from the family nest having followed Edith's development from typist/secretary to journalist/story writer, thinking to herself: First of all, Edith is already going the Chinese route and I don't want merely to hang onto her skirts. Second, the Japanese are much more highly regarded in this society than the Chinese. Third, most people can't tell the two nationalities apart. Therefore, I'll give myself a Japanese identity, research whatever basic information I need, rely on my imagination for the rest, and no one will know the difference. And she was right. 〈. . .〉

Her first novel, *Miss Numè of Japan*, was well received; the *New York Times* reviewer called it "a charming Japanese tale" that gave him "a delightful evening." He found much in it that was "entertaining," praised "the cleverness of incident," and concluded that "it is a well-done piece of writing." Her second book, *A Japanese Nightingale* (1901), was a stunning success. Published by Harper & Brothers, with full color illustrations by a Japanese artist and each page printed on paper decorated with oriental motifs, the book was a visual delight; and the story with its startling twists, its tender emotional subtleties, and mysterious, seductive heroine readily won admirers. 〈. . .〉

As Winnifred Eaton's career continued, with each book following the basic structural formula but tremendously varied in its elaborative details, only the critic of the *Independent* sounded a note of protest, complaining of inaccuracies and saying of one of her novels: "In her latest book *Onoto Watanna* she continues her mistaken career as a Japanese novelist." However, Japanese readers themselves found her work praiseworthy. Kafu Nagai, who studied at Princeton and Rutgers Universities between 1871 and 1873, wrote in his diary about *The Heart of Hyacinth*, "This novel is hardly to be counted among the best literary works, but the style is exquisite and its pretty sentiment is well displayed." Katsuhiko Takeda in *Essays on Japanese Literature* devoted an entire essay to Onoto Watanna and concluded that Onoto Watanna was not a long time resident of Japan; however, in her books "Japanese customs and manners [are] . . . properly introduced to the West"; she is on a par with Lafcadio Hearn and Pierre Loti, and "her descriptions of human feelings are more delicate than those of both famous writers." Apparently then, Winnifred Eaton did do her homework, and furthermore, had enough imagination and skill as a writer, particularly enough knowledge of human nature, to compensate for what she lacked in facts about Japan.

The Onoto Watanna romances are all variations on the theme boy meets girl, boy loses girl, boy finds girl again, but then what romances are not? What is interesting is that her heroines are almost always Japanese or Eurasian young women in socially inferior positions (social outcasts, orphans, unloved stepdaughters) while her heroes are generally American or English men in influential positions (diplomats, ministers, professors, doctors, architects). One might initially conclude that Winnifred Eaton thus catered to stereotypes of the female as childlike, flighty, and brainless while the male was invariably strong and powerful. And further, one might argue that her books supported white supremacist views—little wonder she was popular. However, on closer reading, one notes that the heroines of her novels, though Bohemian and socially unaccepted, are intelligent, independent, and strong-willed. They know what they want and they work to get it with whatever means they possess; generally their means are personal charm, beauty, cleverness, and a good-natured sense of humor. While the men in her novels always hold the purse strings, the women hold the men's heartstrings and manage to get their own way. Thus, Winnifred Eaton's heroines are sturdy survivors, a far cry from the stereotype of the shy, deferential, totally self-negating Japanese female. ⟨. . .⟩

⟨. . .⟩ Her books may not be the work of lasting genius; however, they showed more than a "mediocre talent." And in her last two novels, she returned, in a sense, to her birthright, making use of her father's legacy and the world around her. Her work did not have the refinement and complexity of the work of her friend Edith Wharton, with upper class New York society behind her and European culture before, but in her field of the popular novel, Eaton was highly skilled and always entertaining. Furthermore, the path she chose was politically viable and economically necessary if she was to support herself and four children.

—Amy Ling, "Winnifred Eaton: Ethnic Chameleon and Popular Success," *MELUS* 11, no. 3 (Fall 1984): 8–12

AMY LING

In style and tone, Sui Sin Far's stories ⟨in *Mrs. Spring Fragrance*⟩, like her characters, are unpretentious, gentle, sometimes sentimental. Like other late nineteenth century American women writers, she also wrote stories for children, which make up nearly half of this collection. Through basic human themes— love of men and women, parents and children, brothers and sisters, she draws forth the reader's empathy. What sets her stories apart is her sympathetic portrayal of the Chinese characters living in the United States. Bret Harte had used Chinese characters in his Western stories, but he always presented them from the white man's perspective. Sui Sin Far gave to American letters the Chinese perspective on racial prejudice, economic harassment, and discriminatory immigration regulations. A strident or militant tone was hardly necessary, for she had only to show the situation as it was for the injustice to be apparent; instead, she employed irony. ⟨. . .⟩

Humor is another of Sui Sin Far's weapons, as in the following exclamations by Mrs. Spring Fragrance to her husband, when their Caucasian neighbor's lovelorn son fails to give them his usual greeting: "Ah, these Americans! These mysterious, inscrutable, incomprehensible Americans! Had I the divine right of learning I would put them into an immortal book!" (30). Sui Sin Far is obviously taking delight in the inversion of her Chinese character's appropriating the adjectives commonly used to describe "Orientals" and applying them to whites. The author is also commenting subtly on the supposed superiority—"the divine right of learning"—of those who pass such judgments on other people; the implication here is that the Chinese are not "inscrutable" because of qualities inherent in themselves but because of blind spots in those doing the scrutinizing. Furthermore, Sui Sin Far is taking delight in inverting the character/reader relationship, for a character, who has been made most scrutable, is expressing a desire to write a book about the "inscrutable" white Americans, the reader. We are all comprehensible, of course, to ourselves; it is only the other who is incomprehensible.

Sui Sin Far attempted to reproduce the speech rhythms and patterns of ordinary Chinese Americans in her stories. But her use of literal translations from the Chinese—as in proper names, honorific titles, and axioms—results in a flowery, exotic language somewhat at odds with her purpose of rendering the Chinese familiar to whites, as in the title of the book and in this letter from Mrs. Spring Fragrance to her protégée:

> My Precious Laura,—May the bamboo ever wave. Next week I accompany Ah Oi to the beauteous town of San Jose. There we will be met by the son of the illustrious Teacher, and, in a little Mission, presided over by the benevolent American priest, the little Ah Oi and the son of the Illustrious Teacher will be joined together in love and harmony—two pieces of music made to complete each other. (7)

At other times, the syntax more realistically reproduces Chinese English, as when Lae Choo urges the white lawyer to go to Washington to procure the papers releasing her toddler son from immigration authorities in "In the Land of the Free":

> "Then you go get paper. If Hom Hing not can give you five hundred dollars—I give you perhaps what more that much." (175)

Though Edith Eaton's linguistic portraits may seem at times quaint or strained, her purpose is unfailing: to dramatize the humanness of the Chinese, to draw the reader into their lives, their tragedies, their triumphs. ⟨. . .⟩ Her fiction is comparable to the early stories by Black women, which Carole McAlpine Watson described as "purpose fiction . . . [employing] moral suasion . . . as a conscious strategy of racial self-defense."

—Amy Ling, *Between Worlds: Women Writers of Chinese Ancestry* (Elmsford, NY: Pergamon Press, 1990), 42–44

XIAO-HUANG YIN

While the interracial attraction in this story ⟨"The Smuggling of Tie Co"⟩ is only a secondary theme serving to fortify the image of a self-sacrificing

Chinese girl, it is examined carefully in "The Story of One White Woman Who Married a Chinese" and its sequel, "Her Chinese Husband." As the titles suggest, the two stories tell about an intermarriage from the perspective of an American woman. She contrasts her experiences as the wife of an American and later of a Chinese. By all standards, the stories are quite complex and were considered particularly interesting by critics in Sui's lifetime.

Written in the first person, both stories are narrated by Minnie, an American working girl. She is deserted by her husband James Carson, "a very bright and well-informed" man who thinks she is too ignorant to be his wife. Just when she feels "weary of struggling and fighting with the world" and is about to commit suicide, she is rescued by Liu Kanghi, a Chinese businessman who afterwards marries her. He kindly supports her and does everything to help her recover from the traumatic experience of her previous marriage. As a thoughtful husband, he always treats Minnie with respect and tenderness in sharp contrast to James's callous and brutal conduct. There is not even cultural friction between them. A member of the progressive Reform Club of the Chinese-American community, Liu has been thoroughly Americanized in every respect. In short, as Minnie describes it, their union means "happiness, health, and development" (*Mrs. Spring Fragrance* 134).

Nevertheless, no matter how perfect the marriage is, it runs counter to one of the deepest taboos in American society at the time. The predominant trend in American society then perpetuated racial exclusivity rather than encouraging interracial contacts, as demonstrated by the various anti-miscegenation laws passed at the time and by the treatment of the theme in popular American fiction. ⟨None⟩ of the American stories about Chinese-Caucasian intermarriage written at this time takes a positive tone. Frequently, intermarriage serves as a symbol of "the yellow peril" and as a means of creating a sense of threat to the very survival of the American nation. ⟨. . .⟩ As Minnie mentions in the story, she and her husband have often encountered "sneers and offensive remarks" from the larger society because of their marriage. This is indicative of the strong public disapproval of the couple's behavior, particularly that of Liu. As an "unmarriable Chinaman," he has broken the taboo and "treaded on the forbidden ground." In this sense, Liu's death is inevitable. However, unlike the then-popular American fiction in which the Chinese in love with Caucasians are usually murdered by American mobs, in Sui's story Liu is killed by his own countrymen ⟨. . . .⟩

As a child of a successful intermarriage, Sui's depiction of a Chinese-Caucasian marriage in this way certainly presents a scathing satire on her parents' own romance. On the other hand, although few of Sui's stories of mixed couples have completely happy endings, they contain a different message on a deeper level. In popular American fiction, tragic endings of intermarriages usually symbolize divine trial or punishment to warn that miscegenation is grossly improper and that readers should stay away from such behavior. However, in Sui's stories such endings show how lovers of different races are victimized by the society, thus eliciting sympathy from the public to get rid of the taboo. What sets Sui's stories apart is her favorable description of inter-marriage. Since Liu's marriage with Minnie functions smoothly, it demon-strates that the Chinese have the same feelings as Americans, thus breaking the widespread racist concept that Chinese are incapable of experiencing love, the highest form of sentiment. Furthermore, as the story shows how an American woman exhibits an explicit love for a Chinese man, it stands out as the only truly favorable depiction of marriage between Chinese and whites at the time, thus closing the gap between races.

At this time the truthful depiction of Chinese-Caucasian marriages as they actually existed was still a novelty; getting a factual glimpse into such a union was a rare experience, and to learn of Chinese feelings and lives was a rela-tively new thing. In this sense, Sui's detailed and vivid account of the marriage tells us more about how life was actually led in an early interracial family than a large compilation of factual or sociological material could do. For these rea-sons, "The Story of One White Woman Who Married a Chinese" and "Her Chinese Husband" are among the most significant pieces of Sui's writing.

—Xiao-Huang Yin, "Between the East and West: Sui Sin Far—the First Chinese-American Woman Writer," *Arizona Quarterly* 47, no. 4 (Winter 1991): 69–72

AMY LING

Winnifred Eaton was the author of her own life story in supplying *Who's Who* with the following "facts": born in 1879 in Nagasaki, Japan to a Japanese noblewoman. Her actual birth year was 1875, her birthplace Montreal and her mother, of course, Chinese. In a very literal way, Winnifred created herself, drawing no distinctions between her books and her life, and in fact, extending her fiction-making skills into her life. Her keen marketing instinct and sense of timing were precisely accurate, for orientalism was in full flower at the turn of the century. Her sense of the importance of ethnic validity as manifested in a name, however, was so strong that it overshadowed her belief in her imagi-nation and her storytelling powers, both of which were considerable. ⟨. . .⟩

⟨. . .⟩ Ironically, Edith in asserting her Chinese ancestry was like the English oak, while Winnifred, in assuming a Japanese persona, was more like the bamboo, regarded by the Chinese as a symbol of nobility. What ⟨Roger⟩ Rosenblatt noted as true of Afro-Americans like Malcolm X also held true for Asian Americans like Winnifred Eaton: "Recognizing an elusive and unpre-dictable situation, they adapt to it for survival, becoming masters of both physical and psychological disguise, in part to avoid their hunters" ⟨Black Autobiography: Life as the Death Weapon, 1980, 175⟩.

In Dark Twins, ⟨Susan⟩ Gillman represents "that process of continual self-construction and destruction by someone who is both critic and child of his culture" (13). Though Gillman is writing of Samuel Clemens, this was equally true of Winnifred Eaton. In assuming a Japanese persona, and making liberal use of orientalist materials in her novels, she was a child of her culture and yet, since all was a conscious fantasy and in time a disillusionment, she was a critic of it as well. The dark twin is a trope for the Other within the Self, and the pseudonym is a manifestation of that inner split. Though Gillman recognizes the moral dimensions of imposture, she sees it primarily as a useful strategy for the writer:

> Since "posture" already implies posing or faking, "imposture" is the pose of a pose, the fake of a fake. The word implies no possible return to any point of origin. Synonyms for imposture complicate this ambiguity by distinguishing degrees of intentionality on the part of the impostor. "Deceit" is strongly condemnatory because it refers to "purposeful" deceiving or misleading, whereas "counterfeit" and "fake" may or may not condemn "depending on culpable intent to deceive." Thus imposture raises but does not resolve complex connections between morality and intentionality. Its multiple confusions leave room for lawyers, confidence men, and, ultimately, the writer himself to erase boundaries and circumvent the law, making suspect the premise that knowledge is possible—by legal or any other means. (6)

Further, Gillman writes: "The confidence man presides over the comic tale as hero, not villain. Simon Suggs, a character created by Johnson J. Hooper, another humorist, proclaims in his favorite motto, 'It is good to be shifty in a new country' "(22).

It is crucial to remember that the trickster figure from the perspective of the disempowered is a hero, not a villain. In situations when power is unequal and legally obtained justice is impossible, outsmarting the system is the only means of resistance available. In folk tales of Native Americans and African Americans, the trickster figure—despite what would normally be considered faults—chicanery, cheating, and lying—has the sympathy of the audience because it is through this clever deviousness and deception that unjust situations too large and too difficult for the small person to handle are overcome and victory or a balance of the scales is achieved. In this inversion of established power, the powerless person may take vicarious delight. Furthermore, in contrast to the flexibility and variousness of the trickster, the morally sanctioned stance of his/her opponent at the top of the established hierarchy appears foolishly rigid. Thus, we may read the novels of Onoto Watanna as the brain children of Asian America's first trickster hero.

   —Amy Ling, "Creating One's Self: The Eaton Sisters," *Reading the Literatures of Asian America*, ed. Shirley Geok-lin Lim and Amy Ling (Philadelphia: Temple University Press, 1992), 310–13

ANNETTE WHITE-PARKS

The name appearing on Sui Sin Far's birth certificate is "Edith Maude Eaton," the name appearing on her works as a mature writer is "Sui Sin Far," making it easy to assume that the former identified her role as a child with her family and the latter was taken as a pseudonym for her writing. Textual evidence, though, shows it wasn't that simple, rather that both names, or variations thereof, were part of the writer's identity from early childhood. In her autobiographical "Leaves from the Mental Portfolio of an Eurasian," she relates that a nurse said to her mother, "Little Miss Sui is a storyteller when she was age four." Meaning, in brief, "The Chinese Lily," Sui Sin Far was probably a pet name, given and used by her family. Other details point to the fact that during these first years in England, Sui Sin Far saw herself as an English child, not unlike other children around her ⟨. . . .⟩

   In this context, the writer whom we in the 1990s know as "Sui Sin Far" grew in the 1890s into the public identity of "Miss Edith Eaton," the dutiful, hardworking eldest daughter of an English Canadian family who had to struggle not only with the prejudice leveled against her race and gender, but also with her own constantly flagging health and the burden of family poverty. When her father took her from school at age 11, to sell his paintings and the lace she crocheted herself, on Montréal streets, the older writer recalls that to survive she divided her mind into "two lives" or perspectives, creating a psychic division that underlies both her life and her writing: "I, now in my 11th year; entered into two lives, one devoted entirely to family concerns; the other, a withdrawn life of thought and musing . . ." To the latter, she describes "six keys," among them "the sense of being differentiated from the ordinary by the fact that I was an Eurasian" and "the impulse to create" ⟨*Boston Globe*, 5 May 1912, 6⟩.

   It was the first, practical life, "devoted to family concerns," that would dominate as "Edith Eaton," then one by one her younger siblings, grew into their teens, and the second "withdrawn life of thought and musing" developed where "Sui Sin Far" would continue to flourish. Somehow, between earning a living and caring for 12 younger siblings, the young woman ferreted out cracks of time to launch a newspaper career and begin writing short fiction. Her first located pieces, a series of eight sketches printed in the *Canadian Dominion Illustrated* between 1888 and 1890, were on English and French Canadian subjects and, not surprisingly, were signed "Edith Eaton."

The writer's identification with the Montréal Chinese community seems to have begun sometime in the early 1890s, when she accompanied her mother to "call upon a young Chinese woman who had recently arrived from China as the bride of one of the local merchants" (*Globe*) and recalls that: "From that time on I began to go among my mother's people, and it did me a world of good to discover how akin I was to them." A few years later (1894) when she opened "an office of my own" as a free-lance reporter, her stated purpose was "to fight the battles of the Chinese in the papers." Her evolution during this period into the role of "sympathetic outsider" is evident in that local papers gave her "most of their Chinese reporting" as she fought to champion Chinese Canadians against a growing onslaught of racist laws and practices. The fact that she used the name "Miss Edith Eaton" (listed under "M" in *Lovell's City Directory* 1894–97) indicates that she did not yet see herself as an insider. In an 1896 essay couched as a letter to the editor of the *Montréal Daily Star* (Sept. 21) captioned "A Plea for the Chinaman," she argued brilliantly against raising the Head Tax on Chinese Canadian immigrants from $100 to $500. Yet this letter was still signed as "E.E." ⟨. . .⟩

That by 1900, the writer saw both "Sui Sin Far" and "Edith Eaton" as integral to her personal identity is indicated in her response to a letter from a student at Dartmouth: "Of course I shall be glad to let you have my autograph . . . perhaps I should say *they* as I have both an English and a Chinese name." She closed with both signatures. Though her business identity, signified by correspondence with editors, remained "Edith Eaton" (the practical side of her 11-year-old split), her byline in short stories and in a column for the *Los Angeles Express* becomes by 1904 "Sui Sin Far." In a series for *The Westerner* magazine (based in Darlington, Washington), entitled "The Chinese in America," the editor refers to his author as "Miss Edith Eaton," but describes her Chinese-English parentage in his introduction and uses the byline—*Sui Sin Far* (Edith Eaton). It is notable that in this instance "Sui Sin Far" has been moved to the central, and "Edith Eaton" to the parenthetical position. The culmination of her writings in the book length collection *Mrs. Spring Fragrance* in 1912, and all future fiction, are similarly authored with both names, reflecting, I suggest, the mature writer's growing identity integration.

—Annette White-Parks, "Naming as Identity, Sui Sin Far," *A Gathering of Voices on the Asian American Experience*, ed. Annette White-Parks (Fort Atkinson, WI: Highsmith Press, 1994), 74–78

James Doyle

In spite of her insistence in the *Montreal Star* article on the integration of the Chinese into North American life, Edith Eaton's early fictions tended to exploit exotic and melodramatic images of her mother's people. Her story

"The Gamblers," in the *Fly Leaf* (Feb. 1896), is about intrigue and murder in a gambling and opium den. "The Story of Iso" and "A Love Story of the Orient" in the *Lotus* (Aug. and Oct. 1896) involve star-crossed love and generational conflict in China. "A Chinese Ishmael" (*Overland Monthly* July 1899) is also a melodrama of tragic love, related to the Chinese inability to adapt to the West. In "The Smuggling of Tie Co," (*Land of Sunshine*, July 1900; included in *Mrs. Spring Fragrance*), a Chinese woman disguised as a man dies rather than betray the European-American man who helps her enter the United States illegally from Canada.

But behind the melodrama are indications of Eaton's serious concerns for a subject very close to her own experience, as she revealed in an article for the *Land of Sunshine* (Jan. 1897), "The Chinese Woman in America." Eaton was concerned that women of her ethnicity, when they were able to get into Canada and the United States at all, were frequently subjected to the double discrimination of the archaic domestic attitudes of Chinese men and the racism of European North Americans. The idea of a woman caught between two worlds and unable to participate fully in the lives of either is repeated in much of her fiction. ⟨. . .⟩

⟨. . . Edith Eaton rejected⟩ elaborate but artificial public displays of ethnicity ⟨. . . .⟩ "[People] tell me," Eaton wrote in "Leaves," "that if I wish to succeed in literature in America I should dress in Chinese costume, carry a fan in my hand, wear a pair of scarlet beaded slippers, live in New York, and come of high birth" (132). There is probably a sarcastic allusion here to her sister's career, for in the late 1890s Winnifred Eaton had settled in New York and presented herself publicly in precisely this fashion—except that the costume was not Chinese, but Japanese. ⟨. . .⟩

The fan-and-slippers formula that Edith despised obviously worked for Winnifred ⟨. . . . But⟩ Winnifred eventually became bored with the formulas, and risked trying her hand at other kinds of fiction. Among her non-Japanese works are *Me: A Book of Remembrance* (1915) and *Marion: The Story of an Artist's Model* (1916), both quite successful in their day for their representations of the liberated "new woman"—a character much closer in temperament to Winnifred herself. Although both novels avoid the subject of Asian ethnicity altogether, in the light of other biographical information they provide suggestive glimpses of the family and community tensions that impelled Winnifred Eaton to flee her family, Montreal, and Canada (Ling 27, 32–33). They also reveal a remarkable degree of ironic self-awareness on Winnifred's part, if in *Marion* she is portraying herself in the satirical portrait of Nora Ascough, a would-be writer who mincingly flaunts her newfound independence.

But while Winnifred occasionally dropped the oriental subject matter altogether, Edith continued to use it exclusively in her fiction. ⟨. . .⟩

⟨. . .⟩ Winnifred Eaton Reeve lived on until 1954 ⟨after her sister's death in 1914⟩, enjoying considerable financial comfort as well as vestiges of her early reputation as a novelist. Her work even attained approval in Japan, when a 1970 article by Yoohiro Ando in the Japanese literary journal *The Rising Generation* praised the work of Onoto Watanna as a remarkably astute portrayal of a country and people of which the author had no direct experience (clipping of translation of article, Reeve Papers). There seems little doubt now, however, that Winnifred was the less capable writer of the two sisters. Although she was a fluent stylist while Edith's writing is often stilted and laborious, most of the novels of Onoto Watanna are too obviously dependent on predictable formulas of sentimental fiction, while the stories of Sui Sin Far, whatever their artistic limitations, are sincere efforts to explore important problems of ethnic and gender conflict. But both writers were pioneers among North American writers in adapting Asian subject matter to fiction, and on that basis alone, they both deserve commemoration in Canadian literary history.
—James Doyle, "Sui Sin Far and Onoto Watanna: Two Early Chinese-Canadian Authors,"
Canadian Literature 140 (Spring 1994): 52, 54–57

B I B L I O G R A P H Y

Edith Eaton

Mrs. Spring Fragrance. 1912.

Winnifred Eaton

Miss Numè of Japan. 1899.
A Japanese Nightingale. 1901.
The Wooing of Wistaria. 1902.
The Heart of Hyacinth. 1903.
A Japanese Blossom. 1906.
The Diary of Delia, Being a Veracious Account of the Kitchen with Some Side-lights on the Parlour. 1907.
Tama. 1910.
The Honorable Miss Moonlight. 1912.
Me: A Book of Remembrance. 1915.
Marion: The Story of an Artist's Model. 1916.
Sunny-San. 1922.
Cattle. 1923.
His Royal Nibs. 1925.

Jessica Tarahata Hagedorn

b. 1949

JESSICA TARAHATA HAGEDORN was born in 1949 in Manila, the Philippines, during the regime of Ferdinand Marcos, and she emigrated with her family to San Francisco in 1960. As a poet, novelist, playwright, performance artist, and musician, Hagedorn experiments in form and medium to express the conflicts experienced by Asian immigrants caught between cultures. Like her contemporary, Linda Ty-Casper, Hagedorn speaks against the class inequity and corrupt politics pervading Filipino society; she also takes aim at racism in the United States and develops in her dramas the themes of displacement and the search for belonging.

Hagedorn did not attend college but entered the theater arts training program at the American Conservatory Theatre, where she studied music, acting, martial arts, fencing, and mime. When she was 23, poet Kenneth Rexroth recognized her literary talent and included her poetry in a collection called *Four Young Women*. Also in the early 1970s, Hagedorn founded the West Coast Gangster Choir, an art-rock band whose performances featured interludes written by the artist. By 1980, she had moved to New York with her daughter and published two collections of poems and short fiction, *Dangerous Music* and *Petfood and Other Tropical Apparitions*. In 1988, Hagedorn's dance-theater piece "A Nun's Story" was broadcast on public television's *Alive from Off Center*. The radio drama "Holy Food" was produced in 1989 by WNYC and broadcast nationally. *Dogeaters*, her highly praised novel about urban Manila in the 1970s, was nominated for the 1990 National Book Award.

Hagedorn's oeuvre represents a range of achievement. Humor and wit integrated with a view of the graphic underside of urban life— drug use, physical abuse, murder, ghetto life—characterize her vibrant, at times vitriolic, and uniquely rhythmic poetry, prose, and performance pieces. She remains active in New York theater, where she performs original works like acclaimed multimedia piece "Mango Tango." Her latest novel, *The Gangster of Love*, was published in 1996.

CRITICAL EXTRACTS

JESSICA SAIKI

Reading Hagedorn's poems is to be swept into her pulsating, highly original, often quirky point of view and there is no mistaking her voice for any other poet. She weaves her own world, drawing upon jargon, brand names, TV personalities and the commercial hype bombarding the immigrant to our shores:

> . . . the paranoia/that raised me/and cristina/with her wonderful breasts/stunning the world/in her saks fifth avenue/brassiere or . . . and here we are,/cathedrals in our thighs/banana trees for breasts/and history, all mixed up/saxophones in our voices/when we scream/the love of rhythms/inherent/when we dance

Included are prose selections chronicling the aspirations and eventual disappointments of Pearl and Bong Bong (Antonio Gargazulio-Duarte) in their attempts to make it in America. ⟨. . .⟩

Filipino by heritage, her poems discuss Manila, her origins:

> where the sun is scarlet/like a beautiful slut/ . . . the nuns with headdresses/like wings of doves/beating you/into holy submission/with tales of purgatory/. . . the presidents wife/dictates martial law/with her thighs

This is the tough, street-smart, seen-it-all voice of a survivor. She has an unerring ear for the phony and a discerning mind, listing for America all the traps and materialistic junk held up as necessities of life. The rhythm of her poems, insistent and hypnotic as jungle drums, beats an indelible message into my brain.

The book lives up to its title: these poems sear and smolder. It is a siren call of poetic music that deserves a wide audience.

—Jessica Saiki, [Review of *Dangerous Music*], *Forbidden Stitch: An Asian American Women's Anthology*, ed. Shirley Geok-lin Lim and Mayumi Tsutakawa (Corvallis, OR: Calyx Books, 1989), 241

BLANCHE D'ALPUGET

In the Philippines, "dogeaters" is a slang term for Filipinos. Think of eating dog. Of dog-eat-dog. The people in Jessica Hagedorn's "Dogeaters" have the hunger of emptiness. They're not poor, just empty. They yearn to be filled by *something*. Food, drugs, sex, money: they'll try anything quick and easy. "Dogeaters" is about Manila during the Marcos years.

This flash first novel, as sharp and fast as a street boy's razor, concerns itself with the turbulent trivial people who grow so well in debauched societies. Its characters span the urban social spectrum, ranging from middle-aged commodity billionaires to impoverished teen-agers living off their looks.

In between are hairdressers, movie stars, spoiled wives and children, grandmothers, a general and a gay owner of a decadent disco. The First Lady, not identified, but clearly resembling Imelda Marcos, makes guest appearances in which she spouts lines such as (gesturing to treasures): "Everything you see here is God-given. . . . I am simply here to carry out our Lord's wishes."

Besides hunger, "Dogeaters" is a book about fantasies. While Ms. Hagedorn's people are forever eating—the poor their salted eggs, the rich their spiced pork and Mango Tango ice cream—they dream. There is feeding and fantasy. Feeding on fantasy. Fantasies of feeding. ⟨. . .⟩

⟨. . .⟩ Her novel is written as a scrapbook of memories and precise images of life in Manila from 1956 to about 1985. The chapters of its discontinuous narrative are like fractals, those mathematical forms that present a series of overlapping shapes, endlessly repeated. The whole book is an elegant geometry of chaos. Fantasy and greed change in outward manifestation, remain unchanged within. Space and time spiral deceitfully to stay the same.

The novel offers a picture of ruin at the heart of Philippine society. Two principal characters appear as "I" in "Dogeaters," both mongrels, both with quick minds and sharp tongues, both alienated from their peers, both suffering the pain of clarity in a land of blur.

—Blanche d'Alpuget, "Philippine Dream Feast," *The New York Times Book Review* (25 March 1990): 1, 38

JESSICA HAGEDORN

I first wrote *Tenement Lover* as a song. It became a kind of anthem for my band, which by then was known as The Gangster Choir. The song expressed my reactions to living conditions in New York and my adjustment to the change. ⟨. . .⟩

Doing *Tenement Lover* was the first time I had enough of a budget to realize the visual elements of my work. I had tableaus running through the piece of the bathing beauty character and the guerrilla, the mysterious man scooping up seashells. I also had slides of the Philippines projected, mostly landscapes. The photographer who took them had gone up into the mountains and shot rice fields, sometimes using red filters so that they looked like brilliant-colored abstractions, like landscapes on Mars.

I wanted to communicate to the audience in several ways. There was a visual story with no dialogue spoken, there were Bongbong's letters, there were songs performed live by the band. All these fragments may have seemed disjointed to some people, but by the end you could see the connections.

Tenement Lover turned out to be a very important piece for me. In it I began to explore, with a style that I'm still using, themes that continue to obsess me—otherness, the idea of revolution on many levels, terrorism, dominant culture vs. so-called minority culture. And the idea of home, what homesickness and home mean.

I also wanted to address the political situation in the Philippines. It was important to me at the time, because I hated the Marcos regime. I'm political, and find I'm overtly more political the older I get. I used to dance around that commitment and say, "Let my work speak for myself. It's there, if you want to find it." Now I'll just say yes, I want to include those reflections in my work. I don't pretend to have the answers, but the thing about grappling with politics in art is that the *questions* can be so interesting.

Does my work belong to an Asian-American aesthetic? I think there's a multicultural aesthetic, in the sense that you can draw from many different cultures that have similar experiences. For example, black music really influenced the way I write poetry. Certain rhythms go along with certain forms of jazz and R&B I listen to. But it gets kind of sticky when you try to define these things. I don't want limitations imposed on me.

—Jessica Hagedorn, in *Between Worlds: Plays by Asian Americans*, ed. Theatre Communications Group, Inc. (New York: Theatre Communications Group, Inc., 1990), 77–78

JAIMY GORDON

In her first novel, *Dogeaters*, Jessica Hagedorn creates a working model of the steamily gorgeous, ludicrously corrupt, and passionately derivative popular culture of her native Philippines. From American exile she turns a vision upon its frantic entertainments both x-ray and encyclopedic, and, even so, hers is the glazed eye of the insider. With an insider's troubled disrespect, she names her novel after a pejorative for Filipinos, *dogeaters*, that stresses the visceral and fantastic, for she knows this society literally inside and out.

Her short chapters are a pop culture farrago—radio melodramas, movie scenarios, cafe tables, banquet tables, country club tables, food and more food, a wedding, a beauty contest, clips from *The Metro Manila Daily* or *Celebrity Pinoy*, a gossip tabloid. Her characters are starstruck, even when they are stars themselves, and they love melodrama, for the Philippines have a double colonial legacy: side by side with their mania for American-style glamor is a peculiarly blood-soaked religiosity, the effect of Spanish Catholicism on Filipino fantasy. The plot of *Dogeaters*, when it at last gets under way, embodies a classic Filipino melodrama of blood martyrdom and redemption. 〈. . .〉

〈. . .〉 Characters in melodrama are easy to sum up under the definite article, and a weakness of Hagedorn's prose is its tendency to do just that, to give us "the reclusive beauty queen" and "the starstruck teenager," "the popular Cafe

España," "the beaming President," "the terrified Romeo," "the obsequious young waiter," and "the weeping bride"—flat and stagey epithets of a gossip column or (soap?) opera synopsis. But even these echoes of pop culture seem natural in Hagedorn. ⟨. . .⟩

I've not read anything lately more marvelously alive and exquisitely comic than the opening chapter of *Dogeaters*, which introduces Rio Gonzaga as a schoolgirl, and her poor but determined cousin Pucha, showing off her precocious 36B breasts at *merienda* at the Cafe España after the movies, trying to attract the attention of a rich though repellent boy under the nose of Rio's *yaya* (duenna) Lorenza: "I don't care if he's a little *gordito*, or *pangit*, or smells like a dead goat. That's Boom-boom Alacran, stupid. He's cute enough for me."

In the seven thousand islands of the Philippine Republic, over seventy languages are current, including English, Spanish, Tagalog, and an urban distillation of the three that most of the characters of *Dogeaters* speak and understand. Hagedorn properly salts her portraiture of this polyglot culture with dialect, but leaves an intimidating number of phrases in the text without hint of translation. The headache this gives the reader is real enough, but seems to rise right out of the cacophonous streets full of jeepneys and pedicabs, flowered nylon sun umbrellas and jostling passersby, and is a small price to pay for a splendid ride.

—Jaimy Gordon, "Frantic Entertainments," *American Book Review* 12, no. 5 (November-December 1990): 16, 25

JOHN UPDIKE

A world on quiet fire is arrestingly conveyed by Ms. Hagedorn's episodic, imagistic collage of a novel. A borrowed American culture has given Filipinos dreams but not the means to make dreams come true. As in the novels of the Argentine Manuel Puig, we are reminded how ravishingly Hollywood cinema invaded the young minds of the Third World, where one did not meet the corrective reality of North America upon emerging from the theatre. The popular culture in "Dogeaters" is consumed, like the constantly described food, with a terrible honest hunger. ⟨. . .⟩

"Dogeaters" has a teeming cast of characters, and their multiplicity somewhat dissipates the reader's involvement. The book, prefaced by excessive thanks for help in its composition, feels a bit boiled down, as though its scattered high-energy moments were edited from a more leisurely-paced panoramic work. The Avila family, representing Manila's liberal aristocracy, especially seems skimped, though Senator Avila's assassination is the book's political climax, bringing a number of threads together, and his daughter Daisy's triumph in a beauty contest is its most magic-realist moment. ⟨. . .⟩

Food and romantic fantasies crowd these famished pages. Everybody wants to be loved, especially the torturing general. With little overt editorializing, Ms. Hagedorn sketches a nation that has never had much to be proud of, where even the natives feel like strangers. "Two generations, three generations, it really doesn't matter," Rio's father says. "What matters is I feel like a visitor." ⟨. . .⟩ Though the narrator at the end flies off into a flurry of artiness, including a prayer to the Virgin and a letter from Pucha to Rio Gonzaga as the author of "Dogeaters," Ms. Hagedorn's novel is dense with hard-earned observation. Worried upper-class family life, seamy and hypnotic night life, suffocating and sinister and impotent political life—it is all here, set down with poetic brightness and grisly comedy. The author sees her native land from both near and far, with ambivalent love, the only kind of love worth writing about.

—John Updike, [Review of *Dogeaters*], *The New Yorker* (18 March 1991): 105–106

ROSELLEN BROWN

Hagedorn's first novel—she is a poet and performance artist—is a splashy, vigorous, angry, horrifically amusing and depressing book I'd like to hope represents only a small fraction of Filipino life. Hagedorn's preoccupation is with the corrupt rich, the corrupt politically powerful, and corrupt relations between the sexes, opposite and same. ⟨. . .⟩

The only characters in *Dogeaters* who are not trashed by Hagedorn's jazzy dispassionate fury are the daughter of a reformist senator, who takes to the mountains to join the guerrillas, presumably to give us a faint taste of hope, and Rio herself, whose memories are undermined a bit by Pucha at the end (though why? The book is not about the fickleness of memory; in fact it demands our trust.). It ends with a poetic assertion that the narrator (here the author?) would curse the dangerous island in all the languages of its occupation—Waray, Ilocano, Tagalog, Spanish, English, Portuguese and Mandarin—"but I choose to love you instead."

After so much spilled blood and so many disparaged ideals, I wish Hagedorn had found room for a few more characters whose judgment or honesty we could respect or see as representative of the island she so defiantly loves. (Sympathetic Rio opts out by becoming an adult elsewhere.) What the author has accomplished is a vivid diatribe, more detailed than a cartoon but not much more profound—fascinating, selective in its focus, mordantly funny, hard to feel close to let alone warmed by, but undeniably, luridly instructive. It is more effective as cultural history than as fiction, with whose characters we want to feel more than occasionally implicated. But there's an honorable place for such books—somewhere, I think, between history, poetry and exposé.

—Rosellen Brown, "The Year in Fiction: 1990," *The Massachusetts Review* (Spring 1991): 129, 131–32

SUSAN EVANGELISTA

Hagedorn's novel, *Dogeaters*, nominated for the National Book Award, deals with life in Manila in the 1970's, and makes this reader think of Gabriel García Márquez and *One Hundred Years of Solitude*. In contrast to Márquez, Hagedorn's story is urban-centered (and terribly urbane), moving in a milieu which could only be Manila, with its outrageous blend of Spanish elitism and elegance gone seedy, American flash and decadence, and Third World desperation and brazenness. It is slicing and cutting and irreverent, disjointed like Márquez's dream world, but a little more nerve-tingling than dust-covered Maconda. Nevertheless it carries a strong sense of magic realism, of bizarre characters and strange coincidences, of real life gone unreal with a sudden verbal twist, exposing the reader to "a world totally reconstructed and subverted by fantasy" ⟨Mario Vargas Llosa, "Fiction and Reality," 1987, 5⟩. We are left in limbo between the magic and the real, in a world as it might be described by a peasant, for instance, or a street-boy—someone far removed from the logic and power of that world, experiencing reality but a reality touched with the magic of incomprehension. ⟨. . .⟩

The reader may sense by now that on some levels *Dogeaters* is a disjointed book, with its divergent voices, characters and events. But at the same time we have seen unifying factors: relationships between principle characters, the way they all relate to the major incidents of the novel, especially the assassination of Senator Avila, surely *the* central incident. Joey Sands was there, caught in his own criminal act of robbing his German lover. Romeo Rosales, the slightly pompous innocent who went on believing to the end that he could call on his old high school friendship with Tito Alvarez for aid and succor, was made the scapegoat when the killing needed solution. Romeo, who had been depicted as thinking only of his own vanity, his movie hopes, and his love affair with Trinidad. Rio and Baby Alacran are family friends and class associates of the murdered Senator. Daisy is of course his daughter. La Sultana seems to know about it before it happens, and Cora Camacho does the public commentary every step of the way.

But Hagedorn leaves the connections loosely established; there is nothing neat about this book. And perhaps because of this disjointedness, along with the underlying sense of oneness that the reader gets almost intuitively, the whole thing seems both real and unreal, a little like magic but a little like life. When Gabriel García Márquez was asked to explain some of the more bizarre incidents in *One Hundred Years of Solitude* and some of his other writing, he said that his grandmother used to tell him such stories, in a very down-to-earth, matter-of-fact tone. "Beautiful Remedios rode up to heaven on the sheets one morning." Just so. And this is the feeling one gets from the tone of Hagedorn's novel ⟨. . . .⟩

—Susan Evangelista, "Jessica Hagedorn and Manila Magic," *MELUS* 18, no. 4 (Winter 1993): 42–43, 51

DOLORES DE MANUEL

What does marriage signify in Filipino American fiction? A number of stories and novels, spanning several decades, can be read as addressing the question, both directly and indirectly. The answers constitute a discourse on the economy of marriage, an attempt to determine whether the institution is by nature productive or destructive, fertile or sterile. In working out the equation of value, the fiction of Jessica Hagedorn, Bienvenido Santos, and Linda Ty-Casper quickly brings many factors to the surface. The meaning of marriage depends on where the protagonists have located themselves, and whether this act of self-positioning is conceived in terms that are geographical, racial, cultural, or emotional. It depends on the type of redefinition of social and gender roles that takes place in the act of marriage and union, and whether that redefinition is seen as positive or negative. ⟨. . .⟩

In reading the work of Filipino American fictionists as a running commentary on the economy and imperatives of marriage in the trans-oceanic, cross-cultural setting, a quick definition of traditional Filipino marriage is in order; the easy formula "love, honor, obey" should be supplemented. While noting the high value ascribed to marriage, one should posit, in addition, a code of unspoken, unwritten cultural rules that exist over and above the legal and religious restrictions, including family stability, loyalty, and female subordination. In each work of fiction examined in this paper, one finds that the meanings ascribed to marriage at home in the Philippines shift their ground, as characters move into new territory and come to redefinition.

This shift is most simply and graphically illustrated in Jessica Hagedorn's *Dogeaters* (1990). Rio Gonzaga, a narrator, grows up in the Philippines as an observer of a procession of failed or bizarrely dysfunctional marriages. Her mother, after being humiliated by her husband's flagrant infidelities, attacking him with a pair of spike heels and seeking refuge in the company of homosexual friends, finally moves to America to escape her marriage; Rio comes with her. Her last comment on her own uneasy progress to maturity is "I never marry" (247). For both mother and daughter, the effects of a bad marriage are lasting. Geography is their escape; the ocean between insulates them from the cultural norms of home and enables them to devalue marriage. The novel leaves one questioning whether codes of behavior, gender roles, and social conditions within a macho culture have made marriage in the Philippines an impossibly destructive institution for women, and whether failure is actually an inescapable precondition of its existence.

Although this question is never addressed directly, the novel's conclusion seems to imply that since the rules of marriage are too complicated, it is easier to just get out of the game. Placing oneself outside of the confines of marriage is facilitated by the literal crossing; in this novel America is the escape hatch, the position off the playing board where the rules need not be obeyed. The physical movement allows Rio to step away from the system of value. But the simplicity of this unbinding and redefinition is illusory and deceptive, since decentering and relocation also carry the price of personal destabilization. Rio's description of herself implies a sense of disorientation: "I am anxious and restless, at home only in airports. I travel whenever I can" (247). The act of relocation outside the domain of marriage may imply a permanent dislocation.

—Dolores de Manuel, " 'Across That Ocean Is . . .': Trans-Oceanic Revaluations of Marriage in Filipino American Fiction," *Privileging Positions: The Sites of Asian American Studies*, ed. Gary Y. Okihiro et al. (Pullman, WA: Washington State University Press, 1995), 193–94

B I B L I O G R A P H Y

Dangerous Music: The Poetry and Prose of Jessica Hagedorn. 1975.
Petfood and Other Tropical Apparitions. 1981.
Dogeaters. 1990.
Danger and Beauty. 1993.
Charlie Chan Is Dead: An Anthology of Contemporary Asian American Fiction (editor). 1993.
The Gangster of Love. 1996.

Maxine Hong Kingston

b. 1940

MAXINE HONG KINGSTON was born October 27, 1940, in Stockton, California, the daughter of Chinese immigrants Tom and Ying Lan Hong, who owned and operated a laundry. Aside from attending school and helping with the family business, Maxine spent her free time reading the literary classics her parents had brought from China and attending movies, mostly Chinese operas, at the local Confucian Church. The Kingstons' tradition of passing down myths and family history profoundly influenced the future author, who would incorporate much of these memories into her novels.

In 1962, Maxine graduated from the University of California at Berkeley with a bachelor's degree and married actor Earll Kingston, with whom she has had one son. She then taught high school English and mathematics in California and Hawaii until the publication of her first book, *The Woman Warrior*, in 1976. At the narrative core of the book is Brave Orchid, a fictionalized characterization of Kingston's mother; the text is in fact populated with numerous characters drawn from the Chinese-American community of Kingston's youth. While critical of Chinese traditions, Kingston also disassembles classic stereotypes of Chinese Americans. At once a novel, an autobiography, a fairytale, and an epic poem, *The Woman Warrior* constitutes a genre unto itself. Its original narrative style and exploration of gender and generational conflicts garnered considerable critical acclaim, culminating with the 1976 National Book Critics Circle Award for nonfiction.

In 1980, Kingston published a companion piece to *The Woman Warrior* called *China Men*, in which men are the chief characters. Beginning with the story of the author's father, the poetic narrative explores themes of emigration, ritual, struggle, persecution, and assimilation. Again her literary talents were lauded, and she received the American Book Award for general nonfiction. Her latest novel, *Tripmaster Monkey*, shows off her unique skill of blending, in the words of Herbert Gold in his review for *Tribune Books*, "the kind of magic realism familiar to readers of Latin American fiction with the hard-edged black humor of flower-epoch comic writers and performers."

Kingston's honors include the Anisfield-Wolf Race Relations Award in 1978, the American Library Association Notable Books List in 1980, and the Hawaii Writers Award in 1983. Her poetry and nonfiction articles have been published in academic and mainstream periodicals, including the *English Journal*, *Iowa Review*, *Ms.*, *The New Yorker*, and the *New York Times Magazine*. Kingston has held numerous visiting professorships and continues to lecture at institutions worldwide.

CRITICAL EXTRACTS

SARA BLACKBURN

In this searing, beautiful memoir of growing up as the first-generation American daughter of Chinese immigrant parents, Maxine Hong Kingston illuminates the experience of everyone who has ever felt the terror of being an emotional outsider. It seems to me that the best records of the immigrant experience and the bittersweet legacy it bestows upon the next generation fascinate us because of the insights they provide into the life of the family, that mystified arena where we first learn, truly or falsely, our own identities. It should therefore not be very startling—as it was to me—that this dazzling mixture of pre-revolutionary Chinese village life and myth, set against its almost unbearable contradictions in contemporary American life, could unfold as almost a psychic transcript of every woman I know—class, age, race, or ethnicity be damned. Here is the real meaning of America as melting pot.

Kingston alternates the experiences of her parents and their generation, in China and the Chinatowns of California, with her own. In a starving society where girl children were a despised and useless commodity, her mother had become a physician, then joined her long-ago immigrated husband in America, where she was hence to labor in the laundry which was their survival in the terrifying new land. Their children, raised in the aura of the old myths and their parents' fears for their children and themselves, alternated between revering and despising them. ⟨. . .⟩

In the book's climax, Kingston, now in high school, lashes out at her mother in an extraordinary, liberating tirade in which she claims at last her own shaky identity. And her mother, who once struggled so valiantly for her own, first denies her feelings and then tries to convey the dangers, real and imagined, which have molded her own attitude toward this beloved, maddening stranger. The gap is too wide, for the teenage Maxine has perceived more of her mother's fear than her love, more of her culture's confines than its richness and beauty. The possibilities of love and forgiveness will have to be postponed for the more immediate necessities: the struggles for autonomy, on the one hand, and assimilation on the other. The depiction of these twin struggles is this memoir's great strength.

The Woman Warrior is not without flaws: much of the exquisite fantasy material comes too early in the book, before we're properly grounded in the author's own "reality," and we can appreciate its full impact only in retrospect. There's often a staccato, jarring quality in transition from one scene to another, and we have to work hard placing ourselves in time and event. Prospective readers should not be discouraged by these minor problems. What is in store for those who read on is not only the essence of the immigrant experience— here Chinese, and uniquely fascinating for that—but a marvelous glimpse into the real life of women in the family, a perception-expanding report for the archives of human experience. Praise to Maxine Hong Kingston for distilling it and writing it all down for us.

—Sara Blackburn, "Notes of a Chinese Daughter," Ms. 5, no. 7 (January 1977): 39–40

ANNE TYLER

It becomes apparent fairly early in China Men that this is a less particularized account than The Woman Warrior. The ancestors stand for many other ancestors, for the entire history of Chinese emigration. They farmed cane in Hawaii, built the Central Pacific Railroad across the Sierras ("Only Americans could have done it," officials announced at its completion), or mined gold in Alaska. The author's father entered this country either as a stowaway or as a legal immigrant; both versions are recounted in full, as if they really happened. And there's a chapter on America's Chinese immigration laws from 1869, when this was declared to be a land of "Nordic fiber," through 1978, when at long last the quota system ceased to work specifically against Asians.

But inevitably, the particular triumphs over the general. China, to Maxine Hong Kingston, is "a country I made up." Equally, she makes up her history, her family mythology, coloring it with an artist's eye. Both of her books are nonfiction ⟨. . .⟩ but in a deeper sense, they are fiction at its best—novels, fairytales, epic poems. While the father of the family, preparing to be tested by American immigration authorities, may have had to memorize "another man's life, a consistent life, an American life," his daughter has to memorize a Chinese life. Neither memory, of course, is entirely accurate. Both are creative—sad for the memorizers, perhaps, but all the better for the reader. ⟨. . .⟩

What make the book more than nonfiction are its subtle shifts between the concrete and the mythical. Edges blur; the dividing line passes unnoticed. We accept one fact and then the next, and then suddenly we find ourselves believing in the fantastic. Is it true that when one of the brothers was born, a white Christmas card flew into the room like a dove? Well, possibly; there could be an explanation for that, but . . . . And did it really happen that an uncle lost all his money due to post-hypnotic suggestion—walked the streets in a trance, located a certain stranger in an unfamiliar room, and handed him the contents of his bank account? Does sandalwood grow in phoenix-shaped roots in the caves of lions; does it congeal in the Eastern Ocean as a cicada?

Some of the mythologies are accepted whole from storytelling relatives; others are newly invented by the author's quirky vision. ⟨. . .⟩

The Woman Warrior was startling because of its freshness; it wasn't a book that called to mind any other. *China Men*, of course, lacks that advantage, but it's every bit as compelling as its predecessor. It's a history at once savage and beautiful, a combination of bone-grinding reality and luminous fantasy.

—Anne Tyler, [Review of *China Men*], *The New Republic* (21 June 1980): 33–34

E. M. BRONER

Maxine Hong Kingston has developed a new form. Anthropologists will call it ethnographic. Critics will call it regionalism, the grotesque or gothic. The National Book Award, or the ghost of it, will press it into the category of auto-biography, as they did her first book, *The Woman Warrior*, when it won the NBA. I call *China Men* personal epic.

In the title Hong Kingston uses the pejorative, the patronizing "Chinamen," but she separates the words, perhaps to indicate that this desig-nation is different. These men will not be dealt with pejoratively but hero-ically as the "binders and builders" of Hawaii and the States. This is a book of men, of male ancestry, a counterpart to *The Woman Warrior*, which was the search for self through the untold and told tales of the Chinese family, through the naming and exorcising of ghosts.

That which must be fought through in both books is imposed silence: the aunt in *The Woman Warrior* who cannot tell her tale, the author who, as a shy child, cannot speak in class. *The Woman Warrior* ends triumphantly with the author speaking out and with reference to the legend of a woman poet. The poet was kidnapped and lived among barbarians, yet sang her own songs. When ransomed, she brought back these songs to her people, and the Chinese still sing her words to their instruments. So, in both books, they, in exile, must still remember the words to sing and Hong Kingston is the instrument.

China Men commences with the angry silence of the father, a laundry worker in the land of Gold Mountain (all immigrants call the States "golden"). The daughter chronicler writes, "I think this is the journey you didn't tell me," and she proceeds to "talk story," to imagine-tell for her father. She tells of the arduous test in China given to prospective scholars, to her father's ordeal and his being selected as minor scholar, village schoolmaster to unappreciative boys. ⟨. . .⟩

As the book begins with the teacher father and his unappreciative students, it ends with the brother, a gentle fellow, a remedial-reading teacher to louts who rip books that he buys for the school library. This brother, like all the China Men, has to take his journey into the world of demons. All who are not their own are demons: immigration demons, employer demons, mortician demons, even garbage demons and movie-usher demons. This brother goes into the demonic world of the war in Vietnam, careful, even in war, not to hurt another. When he returns he cannot tell his tale. His sister writes it for him, gives her brother throat and soaring song.

Although the author mentions, in an aside, attending a conference on oral history, this book is not that kind of documentation—the nondramatic, non-selective form of the oral tale. Her work is kinesthetic memory. She takes data and makes it mythopoetic. Her umbilicus branches, encircles, twines around her ancestors. They sprout through her.

—E. M. Broner, "Stunning Sequel to *Woman Warrior,*" *Ms.* 9, no. 2 (August 1980): 28, 30

ELAINE H. KIM

Kingston says that she wrote *The Woman Warrior* and *China Men* together, having conceived of them as an interlocking story about the lives of men and women. But the women's stories "fell into place," and she feared that the men's were anti-female and would undercut the feminist viewpoint. So she collected and published the women's stories in *The Woman Warrior* first, although the men's experiences are no less important and moving to her.

In *China Men*, the narrator, who is again the daughter, is less involved with the characters and far less concerned with relating how she feels about them; Kingston says that *The Woman Warrior* was a "selfish book" in that she was always "imposing my viewpoint in the stories" through the narrator.

Like *The Woman Warrior*, *China Men* expresses the Chinese American experience through family history combined with talk-story, memory, legend, and imaginative projection. But while *The Woman Warrior* portrays the paradoxical nature of the Chinese American experience through the eyes of an American-born Chinese, *China Men* is a chronicle of Chinese American history less particular and less personal. The distance between the narrator and the characters in *China Men* might be attributed to the fact that Kingston heard the men's stories from women's talk-story: ". . . without the female storyteller, I couldn't have gotten into some of the stories . . . many of the men's stories were ones I originally heard from women" ⟨Timothy Pfaff, "Talk with Mrs. Kingston," 1980⟩. ⟨. . .⟩

Despite what some Chinese American male critics of Kingston have alleged, *China Men* is not anti-male; on the contrary, it is the portrait of men of diverse generations and experiences, heroes who lay claim on America for Chinese Americans and who refuse to be silenced or victimized.

China Men is also about the reconciliation of the contemporary Chinese American and his immigrant forefathers, nourished by their common roots, strong and deep, in American soil.

The men and women of *China Men* and *The Woman Warrior* are vivid and concrete refutations of racist and sexist stereotypes. For every No-Name Woman, there is a Fa Mu Lan; for every Great Grandfather of the Sandalwood Mountains, there is a brother in Vietnam. And for each perspective set forth by Maxine Hong Kingston, there is a myriad of other Chinese American viewpoints.

While immigrant and American-born Chinese are reconciled in Kingston through their mutual claim on America, and while Kingston's men and women are survivors, the reconciliation between the sexes is not yet complete. Kingston demonstrates that Asian American writers can depict with compassion and skill the experience of both sexes. A future task is the bringing together of our men and women, in life and in the literature which reflects it.

—Elaine H. Kim, "Visions and Fierce Dreams: A Commentary on the Works of Maxine Hong Kingston," *Amerasia Journal* 8, no. 2 (Fall/Winter 1981): 154–55, 159

SUZANNE JUHASZ

Maxine Hong Kingston's two-volume autobiography, *The Woman Warrior* and *China Men*, embodies the search for identity in the narrative act. The first text places the daughter in relation to her mother, the second places her in relation to her father; they demonstrate how finding each parent is a part of finding oneself. For Kingston, finding her mother and father is to name them, to tell their stories. Language is the means with which she arrives at identity, first at home, and then in the world. But because a daughter's relation to her mother is psychologically and linguistically different from her relation to her father, so is the telling of these stories different.

Although the two texts are superficially similar, they are generated from different narrative patterns. In *The Woman Warrior* alternating movements toward and away from the mother take place within a textual field in which a linear progression, defining first the mother, then the daughter, takes place. In *China Men* narrative movement goes in one direction only, toward the father. But because this impulse in the latter book is continually diffused into generalization and idealization, it begins over, again and again. Such narrative structures suggest the evolution of female identity, which is formed in relation to the mother through the achievement of individuation in the context of connection, in relation to the father through the understanding of separation, the creation of substitutes for connection. Taken together, *The Woman Warrior* and *China Men* compose a woman's autobiography, describing a self formed at the source by gender experience.

To say this is neither to ignore nor to minimize the question of national identity everywhere present in Kingston's writing. Born in the United States to Chinese immigrant parents, her search for self necessarily involves a definition of home. Is it America, China, or some place in between? For Kingston the question of national identity complicates the search for self. Yet it is possible to understand how gender identity and national identity can be versions of one another, how home is embodied in the mother and father who together stand for the primary source of the self. For Kingston, in fact, who has never been there, China is not so much a physical place as it is a construct used by her parents to define their own identities. America too, especially for her parents, is a psychological state as much as it is a place. My own focus ⟨. . .⟩ on sexual identity is therefore not meant to negate the other dimension of the problem, but rather to reveal sexual and national identities as parts of one another. For it is as a Chinese-American woman that Kingston seeks to define herself.

—Suzanne Juhasz, "Maxine Hong Kingston: Narrative Technique and Female Identity," *Contemporary American Women Writers*, ed. Catherine Rainwater and William J. Scheick (Lexington, KY: University of Kentucky Press, 1985), 173–74

LESLIE W. RABINE

In *The Woman Warrior* this conflictual texture ⟨the narrator's ambivalence toward her mother⟩ provides the internal structuring principle; in *China Men* the relationship to the father forms the external framework in which Kingston molds the lives and thoughts of the men in her family and the immigrant community. In *China Men*, the theme of revenge, which permeates the *Woman Warrior*, becomes secondary to the theme of being exiled from home, precisely the theme of the lost paradise, whose absence in *The Woman Warrior* so marked the structure and the female experience recounted. Both books describe with nostalgia the loving rituals accompanying the birth of boys, and both express bitterness over the silence accompanying the birth of girls. Within the texts, these rituals express parental love and make childhood an Edenic place from which girls are excluded. But there are sociohistoric reasons for this difference as well. In *China Men*, the grandfathers and great-grandfathers, admitted to the United States as agricultural and railroad workers, long to go home because the cruel treatment they receive deprives them of a worthwhile life. But in *The Woman Warrior*, the place Maxine's family calls "home" is the country where families sell their daughters into slavery and where daughters-in-law are tortured. "Home" is a place she does not want to go.

Yet Kingston's writing makes permeable this boundary between the apparently mutually exclusive experiences of men and women. Most of the legends incorporated into *China Men* are about exiles who wander in search of returning home, and, in at least two of these legends, exile is symbolized by the men being transformed into women. To be a woman, whose birth is not recognized by the family, is to be a permanent exile, without any home, without a place. To be a man who loses one's home is to cross over into the feminine gender. *China Men*, about men who have been forced to cross over into the feminine gender, is written by a woman, who, in the act of writing, has also, like the woman warrior, crossed over, albeit voluntarily, into the masculine gender and assumed the voice of the men she writes about.

—Leslie W. Rabine, "No Lost Paradise: Social Gender and Symbolic Gender in the Writings of Maxine Hong Kingston" (copyright 1987 by the University of Chicago), in *Revising the Word and the World: Essays in Feminist Literary Criticism*, ed. Vèvè Clark, Ruth-Ellen Boetcher Joeres, and Madelon Sprengnether (Chicago: University of Chicago Press, 1993), 151–52

KING-KOK CHEUNG

⟨In *The Woman Warrior*⟩ Maxine evolves from a quiet listener to a talker of stories. Having transformed the military warrior into a verbal fighter, she recognizes that she herself is a powerful spinner of yarns and not just a receptacle for her mother's tales. Although many chapters of her autobiography are in a sense collaborations between mother and daughter, the daughter becomes increasingly aware of her own contribution, especially in the last section of the book: "Here is a story my mother told me, not when I was young, but recently, when I told her I also talk-story. The beginning is hers, the ending, mine" (240). It is toward the end of this story that the tone noticeably softens. Unlike Brave Orchid, the mother who would "funnel," "pry," "cram," "jam-pack" the daughter with unabated torrents of words, and unlike young Maxine, who has "splinters in [her] voice, bones jagged against one another" (196), adult Maxine modulates her notes to the music of her second tongue, in the manner of Ts'ai Yen, the heroine of her final tale.

Kingston reinterprets the legend of Ts'ai Yen—a poet amid barbarians—and, as she has done with the stories about the no-name aunt and the woman warrior, subverts its original moral. The Chinese version highlights the poet's eventual return to her own people, a return that reinforces certain traditional and ethnocentric Chinese notions ⟨. . . .⟩ Kingston's version, by contrast, dramatizes interethnic harmony through the integration of disparate art forms.

Ts'ai Yen, Maxine's last tutelary genius, resembles but transcends the various other influential female figures in her life. Like Fa Mu Lan, Ts'ai Yen has fought in battle, but as a captive soldier. She engages in another art hitherto dominated by men—writing—yet she does not disguise her sex, thus implicitly denying that authorship is a male prerogative. Like the no-name aunt, Ts'ai Yen is ravished and impregnated; both give birth on sand. But instead of being nameless and ostracized, Ts'ai Yen achieves immortal fame by singing about her exile. Like Brave Orchid, she talks in Chinese to her uncomprehending children, who speak a barbarian tongue, but she learns to appreciate the barbarian music. The refrain of this finale is reconciliation—between parents and children, between men and women, and between different cultures.

It is by analogy to Maxine—alienated alike from the Chinese world of her parents and the world of white Americans—that Ts'ai Yen's full significance emerges. The barbarians attach primitive pipes to their arrows, which thereby whistle in flight. Ts'ai Yen has thought that this terrifying noise is her nomadic captors' only music, until she hears, issuing night after night from those very flutes, "music tremble and rise like desert wind" ⟨. . . .⟩ Recalling young Maxine's ambivalence toward language (because it is frequently associated with dominance), an ambivalence that is in a sense reinforced by the lethal text on the warrior's back, we can appreciate all the more the poet's alternative mode of expression. The American language, Maxine discovers, can send forth not just terrifying "death sounds"—threats, insults, slurs—but stirring tunes. Caught in a cross-cultural web of Eastern and Western chauvinism, Maxine too conveys sadness and anger through high-sounding words. She does not (and does not want to) return to China, but she reconnects with her ancestral culture through writing. Instead of struggling against her Asian past and her American present, she now seeks to emulate the poet who sings to foreign music. Not only have her Chinese materials and imaginings "translated well," in the course of such creative translation she has achieved an inner resolution. As the lyrical ending intimates, Maxine has worked the discords of her life into a song.

—King-Kok Cheung, "'Don't Tell': Imposed Silences in *The Color Purple* and *The Woman Warrior*," *PMLA* 103, no. 2 (March 1988): 171–72

AMY LING

Maxine Hong Kingston's *Woman Warrior* was deservedly recognized for its boldness, power, and beauty, its fullness of voice in expressing the hyphenated condition, but this work did not spring full blown from the empyrean. Most of the writers we have examined, despite the Chinese tradition of repression of women, were also outspoken and individualistic. Nearly all their works have been ignored—in many cases, as I hope to have shown, undeservedly so. Looking back, we find that the works that received accolades in their time— Winnifred Eaton's romantic confections, Jade Snow Wong's autobiography— reflected more their audience and its taste than the quality of the books themselves. The frail Japanese or Eurasian heroines romantically involved with dominant Caucasian men in high positions, the Chinese American success story at a time when the United States was at war with Japan, satisfied a public that sought to confirm its own myths, in stories about its superiority, generosity, and openness. It was not particularly interested in learning about the Chinese themselves or in dispelling stereotypes. In fact, to a large extent, it still finds them "inscrutable."

In "Cultural Mis-Readings by American Reviewers," Kingston expresses her frustration that two-thirds of the critics who praised her book could not see beyond their own stereotyped thinking; she cites examples of the painful "exotic-inscrutable-mysterious-oriental reviewing." Here is one example, from the *Chattanooga News–Free Press*:

> At her most obscure, though, as when telling about her dream of becoming a fabled "woman warrior" the author becomes as inscrutable as the East always seems to the West. In fact, this book seems to reinforce the feeling that "East is East and West is West and never the twain shall meet," or at any rate it will probably take more than one generation away from China. (63)

The inscrutableness, it seems to Kingston and to me, is in the eyes of the beholder, and the unbridgeable gulf as well. Chinese Americans have been explaining themselves for nearly a century, but their voices are either ignored or misunderstood.

A major theme in Kingston's *Woman Warrior* is the importance of articulateness. Finding one's voice and telling one's stories represents power, just as having one's stories buried is powerlessness. From the first episode, "No Name Woman," in which Kingston disobeys her mother's injunction and tells the story of the prodigal aunt whom she calls her "forerunner," through the accounts of her own childhood (her belief that her mother had cut her frenum, her silence in Caucasian school, her terrible bullying of a Chinese American classmate in an effort to make her speak—an act of self-hatred), to the last episode, "A Song for a Barbarian Reed Pipe," Kingston elaborates on this theme. Instead of the confusion and humiliation about her Chinese background that she felt as a child, she now finds, in the stories and customs that set her apart from her Caucasian classmates, her heritage and treasure, her strength and identity. Kingston's work combines the traits of the Chinese American writers who preceded her—protest, storytelling, nostalgia, and experimentation. The effect is one of surprising power and startling beauty.

—Amy Ling, "Chinese American Women Writers: The Tradition behind Maxine Hong Kingston," *Redefining American Literary History*, ed. A. LaVonne Brown Ruoff and Jerry W. Ward, Jr. (New York: Modern Language Association of America, 1990), 235–36

SIDONIE SMITH

⟨No⟩ single work captures so powerfully the relationship of gender to genre in twentieth-century autobiography as Maxine Hong Kingston's *Woman Warrior*.

⟨. . . It⟩ is, quite complexly, an autobiography about women's autobiographical storytelling. A post-modern work, it exemplifies the potential for works from the marginalized to challenge the ideology of individualism and with it the ideology of gender. Recognizing the inextricable relationship between an individual's sense of "self" and the community's stories of selfhood, Kingston self-consciously reads herself into existence through the stories her culture tells about women. Using autobiography to create identity, she breaks down the hegemony of formal "autobiography" and breaks out of the silence that has bound her culturally to discover a resonant voice of her own. Furthermore, as a work coming from an ethnic subculture, *The Woman Warrior* offers the occasion to consider the complex imbroglios of cultural fictions that surround the autobiographer who is engaging two sets of stories: those of the dominant culture and those of an ethnic subculture with its own traditions, its own unique stories. As a Chinese American from the working class, Kingston brings to her autobiographical project complicating perspectives on the relationship of woman to language and to narrative.

Considered by some a "novel" and by others an "autobiography," the five narratives conjoined under the title *The Woman Warrior* are decidedly five confrontations with the fictions of self-representation and with the autobiographical possibilities embedded in cultural fictions, specifically as they interpenetrate one another in the autobiography a woman would write. For Kingston, then, as for the woman autobiographer generally, the hermeneutics of self-representation can never be divorced from cultural representations of woman that delimit the nature of her access to the word and the articulation of her own desire. Nor can interpretation be divorced from her orientation toward the mother, who, as her point of origin, commands the tenuous negotiation of identity and difference in a drama of filiality that reaches through the daughter's subjectivity to her textual self-authoring.

Preserving the traditions that authorize the old way of life and enable her to reconstitute the circle of the immigrant community amidst an alien environment, Kingston's mother dominates the life, the landscape, and the language of the text as she dominates the subjectivity of the daughter who writes that text. It is Brave Orchid's voice, commanding, as Kingston notes, "great power" that continually reiterates the discourses of the community in maxims, talk-story, legends, family histories. As the instrument naming filial identities and commanding filial obligations, that voice enforces the authority and legitimacy of the old culture to name and thus control the place of woman within the patrilineage and thereby to establish the erasure of female desire and the denial of female self-representation as the basis on which the perpetuation of patrilineal descent rests. Yet that same voice gives shape to other possibilities, tales of female power and authority that seem to create a space of cultural significance for the daughter; and the very strength and authority of the maternal voice fascinates the daughter because it "speaks" of the power of woman to enunciate her own representations. Hence storytelling becomes the means through which Brave Orchid passes on to her daughter all the complexities of and the ambivalences about both mother's and daughter's identity as woman in patriarchal culture.

> —Sidonie Smith, "Maxine Hong Kingston's *Woman Warrior*: Filiality and Woman's Autobiographical Storytelling," *Feminisms: An Anthology of Literary Theory and Criticism*, ed. Robyn R. Warhol and Diane Price Herndl (New Brunswick, NJ: Rutgers University Press, 1991), 1058–59

SHIRLEY GEOK-LIN LIM

What marks Kingston's memoirs as literary is the way in which "naming" or language figures in her work to deconstruct and deny any single reality of Chinese American female identity. What marks it as feminist is its persistent constructions and reproductions of female identity, the continuous namings of female presences, characters, heroines, and figures. No Name Woman is the first of these figures (and behind No Name Woman the storyteller/mother), a victim valorized by the narrator as hero. In this first narrative act, the narrator's self-conscious "writing" is presented as a rescue of the ancestor from the punishment of silence. No Name Woman's name is itself an oxymoron. She has no name, but the narrator in naming her No Name Woman has given her a name. No Name Woman's identity is that of lack, her presence inscribed in her absence. No Name Woman is a figure for woman as that which is displaced by man and from man, a gap in the his-storical memory. But the act of writing is itself not unambiguous; the rescue into memory through writing is after all a testimony to No Name Woman's sins, and the opening chapter closes on the instability of the writer's position in the feminist project of reclaiming a matrilineal genealogy: "My aunt haunts me—her ghost drawn to me because now, after fifty years of neglect, I alone devote pages of paper to her. . . . I do not think she always means me well. I am telling on her" (16).

The ambivalence of relationship between writer and ancestor echoes the ambivalences between narrator/daughter and mother. The maternal discourse informs the daughter, producing such strong female figures as the swordswoman, Fa Mu Lan: "When we Chinese girls listened to the adults talking-story, we learned that we failed if we grew up to be but wives or slaves. We could be heroines, swordswomen" (19). Or the figure of the shaman, the mother as midwife and healer. But it also deforms the daughter: "My mother has given me pictures to dream—nightmare babies that recur, shrinking again and again to fit in my palm" (86). The discourse is disturbingly female, of "nightmare babies," and it is also racial: "To make my waking life American-normal, I turn on the lights before anything untoward makes an appearance. I push the deformed into my dreams, which are in Chinese, the language of impossible stories (87). Race and gender intersect in the daughter's response to her Chinese mother's talk-stories, as do form and deformity, language and dream, American and Chinese. Chinese is "the language of impossible stories," impossible because the dreams are nightmares, because the language is Chinese in an "American-normal" life, and because the reality of that dream-Chinese language is denied (as No Name Woman was denied) in the American-normal waking life. The mother's talk-stories are in Chinese (Cantonese), and the narrator, head stuffed "like the suitcases which they jam-pack with homemade underwear," is engaged in the project of disburdening herself of them. As with No Name Woman, the narrator is "telling" on her mother who "does not always mean me well."

The narrator's self-consciousness about her writing (storytelling) is a consistent thread in the book which she picks up in various metaphors. One figure is that of the forbidden stitch, that knot of embroidery so fine that in sewing it thousands of embroiderers reputedly lost their sight. The narrator claims: "There was one knot so complicated that it blinded the knotmaker. Finally an emperor outlawed this cruel knot, and the nobles could not order it anymore. If I had lived in China, I would have been an outlaw knotmaker" (163). The knot is what the narrator makes, a figure so tightly and complexly interwoven that its making leads to blindness. The metaphor of the knot covers the making of the mother/daughter relationship in the text, a figure so tightly and complexly tied that the greatest skill will be needed to unknot it. In China the knots were made into buttons, frogs (fasteners), and bellpulls, figures of joining, tying, connection, and sound. The metaphor of the knot leads to the story of the mother cutting the daughter's tongue. The image is of silencing, but it is actually the frenum the mother cuts "so that you would not be tongue-tied" (164). The mother cuts the knot so the daughter can speak, in a figure which paradoxically conveys both silencing and speech; the daughter's desire is to be a knotmaker, a figure for art and affiliation. The daughter's empowerment by maternal action and discourse is expressed in these series of figures, together with the powerful ambivalences of response that these figures produce: "Sometimes I felt very proud that my mother committed such a powerful act upon me. At other times I was terrified. . . . 'Did it hurt me? Did I cry and bleed?' " (164). The mother is informing and deforming power; the reinscribing of maternal talk-stories, of oral into written speech, is the daughter's act of appropriating the power of the maternal discourse for herself.

> —Shirley Geok-lin Lim, "The Tradition of Chinese American Women's Life Stories: Thematics of Race and Gender in Jade Snow Wong's *Fifth Chinese Daughter* and Maxine Hong Kingston's *The Woman Warrior*," *American Women's Autobiography: Fea(s)ts of Memory*, ed. Margo Culley (Madison, WI: University of Wisconsin Press, 1992), 261–62

Donald C. Goellnicht

The social and psychological repercussions of the exclusion laws on Chinese and Chinese American men were tremendous, and they have been documented by a number of historians and sociologists ⟨including Stanley Sue, Nathaniel Wagner, and Reed Ueda⟩. Elaine Kim has pointed out that with job opportunities scarce and women absent in the "bachelor" Chinatowns—ghettoes where Chinese and Chinese American men were forced to live—some of these men ended up, against their will, in traditionally "women's" jobs, as waiters, launderers, servants, and cooks. In "The Father from China" Hong Kingston presents her father and his partners as engaged in their laundry business for long periods each day—a business considered so low and debased that, in their songs, they associate it with the washing of menstrual blood, which links their occupation back to Tang Ao, whose foot-binding bandages smelled like menstrual rags when he was forced to wash them ⟨*China Men*, 4⟩. ⟨. . .⟩ At night, these "bachelors" engage in more "woman's work": they cook their own meals and hold eating races, with the loser washing the dishes. The absence of wives is stressed, but this has to do as much with the difficulty of taking on the menial tasks women would usually perform as with a sense of emotional deprivation. Once Brave Orchid—Ed/BaBa's wife from China—arrives in New York, the traditional roles resume: she cooks, cleans, and washes for the men. Once again, the female narrator sympathizes with these fathers but also critiques traditional gender roles.

Most criticism is leveled, however, at the dominant racist society. In what appears a deliberate attempt to trap China Men in the stereotypical "feminine" positions it had assigned them, American society perpetuated the myth of the effeminate or androgynous "chinaman," while erasing the figure of the "masculine" plantation worker or railroad construction worker. We are all familiar with the stereotype of the Chinese laundryman or waiter, but few know that the railroads so essential to development in North America were built with large numbers of Chinese laborers, who endured tremendous hardship and isolation in the process, or that Hawaiian sugar plantations were carved out of tropical forests with Chinese labor. ⟨. . .⟩

Hong Kingston seeks to redress this wrong of stereotyping and historical erasure, not by a simple reversal ⟨of⟩ the figure of laundryman/cook and that of railroad laborer/plantation worker, "feminine" and "masculine," respectively, but by a disruption of this gendered binary opposition—as we find in the Tang Ao and Tu Tzu-chun myths—which shows both roles and both job types to entail hardships and rewards. To this end she presents us with a variety of China Men from her family: Bak Goong, her "Great Grandfather of the Sandalwood Mountains," who endured the physical hardships of being a sugar plantation worker in Hawaii but who was also "a fanciful, fabulous man" (110); Ah Goong, her "Grandfather of the Sierra Nevada Mountains," a railway construction worker who risked his life from a suspended basket to set gunpowder charges in the mountains but whose intense loneliness at being a married "bachelor" finds expression in his nocturnal reveries on the myth of the Spinning Girl and her Cowboy (129); and BaBa, her father, the Chinese scholar who becomes an American laundryman. These generations of men are presented in all their pain and dignity.

—Donald C. Goellnicht, "Tang Ao in America: Male Subject Positions in *China Men*," *Reading the Literatures of Asian America*, ed. Shirley Geok-lin Lim and Amy Ling (Philadelphia: Temple University Press, 1992), 197–99

STEPHEN H. SUMIDA

As elsewhere in missionaries' campaigns to convert "heathen" people, in California the act of teaching English literacy to rescued women was aimed at enabling the converts not only to read the Bible but also to confess their sinful, pagan pasts and to make way for a new Christian life. Whatever the Chinese American convert's past, it was thus intertwined with a culture their "rescuers" considered not simply inferior, but sinful. Writing such an "autobiography" for the missionaries had to be quite different from the "confessing" to people of the same culture; for the Chinese woman autobiographer—to save her very life, if she had been a caged prostitute in San Francisco—had to deal with how she would, by her writing, be considered a representative of her culture for an audience that believed their own culture and notions of individual virtue to be superior to hers. In such an autobiography, a confession implied an apology to a higher authority.

Chinese American autobiography today inherits this history. By 1976 when Maxine Hong Kingston's *The Woman Warrior: Memoirs of a Girlhood Among Ghosts* was published, some Asian American writers and literary critics, notably Frank Chin and his fellow editors of *Aiiieeeee! An Anthology of Asian-American Writers* (1974), were raising questions about how Asian American first-person narratives affirmed, suggested ignorance of, or were indifferent to cultures and literary histories not only of racist depictions of Asians but also of coaching books and converts' autobiographies and the like. Kingston's book could be seen and judged as an attempt at two things, perhaps both at once: It could be a critique of its narrator, a fictional first-person "I" meant to be questioned so that her confusions about Chinese American identity and the causes and consequences of her American ignorance of China might be understood; or the book could be entirely "transparent," not an interplay of hiding and revealing but a clear revelation by means of explicit, descriptive statement of what it means to grow up Chinese American and female. The selling of *Woman Warrior* as nonfiction, a marketing practice that continues today, tended to throw weight and judgment heavily on the side of the latter interpretation, so despite Kingston's disclaimers that she was not "representing" but had made very significant changes in retelling them, certain stories are generally believed to be nonfictional, transmitted as directly from Chinese tales as oral traditions allow. Contrary to many reviews that took her versions for granted, Kingston implicitly questioned how a daughter would interpret her mother's Chinese culture, given the American contexts, in which they both live, of idealism and racism, sexism, and cultural, historical ignorance. So, for instance, in "White Tigers," the narrator's belief that a woman was proscribed from being a warrior is a reflection on and critique of the prohibition in the American military, during the time the narrator is growing up, against women entering combat. The book's title, meanwhile, proclaims that unlike in America, in the mother's culture there *are* women warriors, exceedingly well-known military ones. Kingston herself has made it explicit that she considers a critique of the book's narrator and her constructs of American and Chinese cultures a key to its reading. *The Woman Warrior* in this way is a Chinese American woman's *Bildungsroman*, a narrative not aiming to present how China, Chinese, and Chinese Americans essentially are, but to plot the imaginative, psychological, ethical, and bodily development of its main character, the narrator herself. The work is, in short, an example of "growing up Asian American" in anything but a simplistic sense.

    —Stephen H. Sumida, "Afterword," *Growing Up Asian American: An Anthology*, ed. Maria Hong (New York: William Morrow and Company, Inc., 1993), 402–3

B I B L I O G R A P H Y

The Woman Warrior: Memoirs of a Girlhood among Ghosts. 1976.
China Men. 1980.
Hawaii One Summer. 1987.
Tripmaster Monkey: His Fake Book. 1988.

Joy Kogawa

b. 1935

JOY KOGAWA was born Joy Nakayama in Vancouver, British Columbia, on June 6, 1935. Her parents, Lois Yao Nakayama and Gordon Goichi, were first-generation Japanese immigrants; her father was a Christian minister, and her pious upbringing resonates in the religious symbolism and clergy figures that appear in her fiction. After high school, Joy took courses at the University of Alberta, Anglican Women's Training College, the Conservatory of Music, and the University of Saskatchewan. While building her writing career, Joy worked as a staff writer for the Office of the Prime Minister in Ottawa, Ontario, from 1974 to 1976. At 22, she married David Kogawa, with whom she had two children before the couple divorced in 1968.

Kogawa's first three books, *The Splintered Moon*, *A Choice of Dreams*, and *Jericho Road*, were collections of poetry not widely distributed in the United States. Then, in 1981, *Obasan*, her novel about the Japanese-Canadian internment experience, was published to wide critical acclaim. *The New York Times Book Review* hailed it as a "tour-de-force . . . brilliantly poetic in its sensibility." It received the Canadian Authors' Association Book of the Year Award and the first annual Books in Canada Novel Award, and it has since been taught in litera-ture and social sciences courses throughout North America. Kogawa also brought the story of Naomi, the protagonist of *Obasan*, to chil-dren in *Naomi's Road*, published in 1986.

Itsuka followed in 1992, continuing the story of *Obasan*'s now matured narrator and set in Toronto during the 1980s, when Japanese Canadians fought for and won recompense from the federal govern-ment for their treatment during World War II. Like *Obasan*, this his-toriographic novel is a passionate redress against history, a call for breaking free of imposed silences and for finding a sense of belonging.

Kogawa has held several writer-in-residence positions at Canadian universities and currently lives in Toronto.

CRITICAL EXTRACTS

ERIKA GOTTLIEB

Since the entire book ⟨*Obasan*⟩ is a document of silence turning into sound, we become intensely aware of the burden carried by language in this invocation of the consciousness of a silent people. To say that Joy Kogawa has a language of her own is not sufficient. Many good poets or writers do achieve that. But in Naomi's narration one often has the feeling that the writer is virtually reinventing language. Unmistakably, the style is the result of extensive linguistic experimentation, presenting us with the special flavour of Japanese Canadian speech patterns and their underlying sensibilities. The writer translates Japanese expressions, often including the Japanese turn of thought. Occasionally she mixes English words with Japanese: "Nothing changes me, I say."

Yet none of these devices can explain the suggestive cadences of the dialogue, for example, when Uncle is looking at the thirty-six-year-old Naomi: "Too young . . . Still too young." There are a lot of passive constructions: we cannot see, we cannot know the source of action. What is visible is only the subject acted upon. "Too much old man," he says and totters back . . . "Mo ikutsu? What is your age now?" And when the old people refuse to give answers to Naomi's repeated questions, their evasions sound like age old proverbs—"Everyone some day dies," or "Still young, too young. Some day."—that have to be decoded, solved like a riddle to get to the true meaning. The truncated sentences have their own slow movement: "Burredo. Try. Good." Some sentences consist of nouns without verbs, or only of adjectives: "Now old," Obasan reports. "Everything old." Yet, in the hands of the skilful narrator-recorder this elliptical, barren language reminds the reader of the poetic quality of child's language, or of Shelley's definition of the language of the poet-Maker: it is vitally metaphorical.

The descriptions have a concrete, literal, imagistic quality. Yet, the poet-writer's strategies are also quite consistent in guiding our response to the world she presents. First she would carefully describe the natural phenomenon, creating an image in its "sensuous particularity." Then she proceeds to make further use of this image just created by relating it to the human world. By this method she assumes a fairly extensive control over our response. To look at one example: after Uncle's death, Obasan and Naomi go up to the attic to look for some old family documents, and they see a spider's web:

> As she pushes a box aside, she stretches the corner of a spider's web, exquisitely symmetrical, balanced between the box and the magazines. A round black blot, large as a cat's eye, suddenly sprouts legs and ambles across the web. Shaking it . . . I recoil, jerking my arm up, sending the beam of light over the ceiling and a whole cloudy scene of carnage. Ugh! What a sight! A graveyard and feasting ground combined . . . But we're trapped, Obasan and I, by our memories of the dead—all our dead—those who refuse to bury themselves. Like threads of old spider webs, still sticky and hovering, the past waits for us to submit, or depart. When I least expect it, a memory comes skit-

tering out of the dark, spinning and netting the air, ready to snap me
up and ensnare me in old and complex puzzles.

By now the conceit—the extended metaphor of man ensnared by the past as
the poor insect is ensnared by the imperceptibly fast formation of the spider
web—is taking shape in front of our eyes. It is an association the writer is test-
ing out in its various aspects, but an association built on an image she had first
created for us to see and touch—an earned association. And by weaving the
metaphor with us, she also engages us in the puzzle, the central puzzle in
Naomi's life:

> Just a glimpse of a worn-out patchwork of quilt and the old question
> comes thudding out of the night again like a giant moth. Why did
> my mother not return? After all these years, I find myself wondering,
> but with the dullness of expecting no response. "Please tell me about
> Mother," I would say as a child to Obasan. I was consumed by the
> question. Devoured alive.

The literal, down-to-earth associations behind the "complex puzzles" make it
truly exciting that the narrator is "devoured alive." There is an imperceptible,
sinister, extremely able spider working somewhere in the cosmos to set up
these intriguing puzzles, and together with the narrator we are compelled to
seek answers.
—Erika Gottlieb, "The Riddle of Concentric Worlds in *Obasan*," *Canadian Literature* 109
(Summer 1986): 39–40

LYNNE MAGNUSSON

There is a silence that cannot speak.
　There is a silence that will not speak.
　Beneath the grass the speaking dreams and beneath the dreams is a
sensate sea. The speech that frees comes forth from that amniotic
deep. To attend its voice, I can hear it say, is to embrace its absence.
But I fail the task. The word is stone.

What does it mean to attend a voice by embracing its absence? And why does
a novel that finds such adequate language for a story of suffering persistently
question the adequacy of words? Joy Kogawa's *Obasan* has rightly been cele-
brated for its power as a political speech act, as a strong protest against the
treatment of Japanese Canadians in the years of and following the Second
World War. What has received less attention is Kogawa's pervasive concern
with the act of speech itself. Naomi's individual drama is closely caught up in
her linguistic anxiety, which comes to serve as a synecdoche for her estrange-

ment—from others, from her cultural origins, from the absent mother who preoccupies her thoughts, from her past.

Reasons for Naomi's distrust of words are not hard to find—some commonplace, others particular to the circumstances of Naomi's upbringing. Revelations of the kind the novel builds toward—the private aftermaths of the Nagasaki bombing—we are accustomed to think of as "unspeakable." And the printed words—newspaper clippings—in Aunt Emily's file about the working conditions of the Japanese Canadians in the beet fields of southern Alberta—"Grinning and happy"—are far removed from the child Naomi's ordeal on the Barkers' farm. Not only do the official accounts in print—all that were available to Aunt Emily, removed in Toronto from the actuality of the suffering in Granton—misrepresent Naomi's experience, but Naomi herself cannot find words to tell Emily: "I cannot tell about this time, Aunt Emily. The body will not tell" (196). It is not just that to find words is to retrace the pain; language seems to yield only a shallow evocation of intense experience. Furthermore, these commonplaces about what language cannot adequately express are characteristically the rhetorical servants of the writer's adequate expression. Speaking of something as inexpressible has the effect of intensifying what is expressed. For the skilful writer, deprecating the adequacy of words is more often a strategy for expression than an admission of failed expression.

Direct references to inexpressibility are by no means Kogawa's sole resource for emphasizing this pervasive concern. The struggle to hear and the struggle to speak are not merely the *content* of the proem whose opening lines I have quoted above. The *style* of the proem and—equally—the style of many sequences of the novel itself bespeak an effort at speech. The characteristic style is poetic and imagist rather than novelistic or discursive. The images of the proem progress with a dreamlike fluidity through association, with the linkages not fully articulated for the reader. Neither is the connection between the first and second sentences made explicit:

> There is a silence that cannot speak.
> There is a silence that will not speak.

The reiterative structure of the short sentences places emphasis on the difference between "cannot" and "will not"; but the reader, without the guidance of logical indicators, is left to determine whether two silences are being distinguished or whether an initial formulation of an elusive proposition is being reformulated. Also notable are the universalizing use of the definite article ("the dreams," "the speech," "the word," "the stone," "the sealed vault," "the seed flowers"), "the speech" and "voice" attributed to no specified speaker, the disembodied "I" (Naomi? Kogawa?): the language of the proem is indeterminate and, perhaps, for the reader, indeterminable. The writer's words, as tracks of the writer's meaning, are almost as elusive as the voice and words pursued in the writing: "The sound I hear is only sound. White sound. Words, when they fall, are pock marks on the earth. They are hailstones seeking an underground stream." Some might attribute the pictorial and disjunctive qualities noted here to Kogawa's poetic vocation, or to her Japanese cultural and linguistic heritage, and consider that a sufficient explanation. But Kogawa can and does vary her style, easily managing—for example—a direct and colloquial style in the diary entries of Aunt Emily. This suggests that variations in style within the novel are motivated by the desire to achieve particular rhetorical effects. In the proem Kogawa creates for the reader a model of reading analogous to the experience with words that is being described; that is, the style acts out the content.

—Lynne Magnusson, "Language and Longing in Joy Kogawa's *Obasan*," *Canadian Literature* 116 (Spring 1988): 58–59

MASON HARRIS

The remarkable success of Joy Kogawa's documentary novel ⟨*Obasan*⟩ in weaving historical fact and subjective experience into a coherent whole is partly due to its ability to co-ordinate several layers of time around a single event: the internment and dispersal of the Japanese Canadians during and after the Second World War. The most obvious purpose of the novel is to reconstruct a suppressed chapter in Canadian history—this is Aunt Emily's special project. In counterpoint to Emily's facts and documents stands the intense personal history of Naomi's narrative, which reveals the damage inflicted on a child by the destruction of her community. As the narrative unfolds we become aware of another layer of history: that of the succeeding generations through which an immigrant community adjusts to a new culture, and the disruption of the relation between these generations by the dispersal of the Japanese Canadian community. Aunt Emily provides the essential facts, and Naomi's record of inner experience invites the reader to a strong emotional involvement in the narrative, but it is the history of the generations, as represented by the Kato and Nakane families, which binds together the various time-layers of the novel. ⟨. . .⟩

In all immigrant communities the first, second, and third generations represent crucial stages in adjustment to the adopted culture. The importance of these generations in the Japanese Canadian community is indicated by the fact that they are given special names: *Issei* (immigrants from Japan), *Nisei* (the first generation born in Canada), and *Sansei* (the children of the *Nisei*). In the novel, Obasan and Uncle Isamu represent the Issei, while Emily comes from the political side of the Nisei. Though Naomi is a Sansei by birth, the fact that she was raised by an immigrant aunt and uncle puts her more in the cultural situation of the Nisei, but without politics or community.

Emily and Naomi are drawn together by a mutual need to heal the breach the destruction of their community has opened between Nisei and Sansei generations. Emily pursues this goal actively over twenty years, with amazing persistence considering her niece's lack of response, while in the course of the novel Naomi gradually comes to recognize her need for the values her aunt conveys to her from the ideals of her own generation, so cruelly defeated by history. ⟨. . .⟩ In reconstructing her past under Emily's influence, ⟨Naomi⟩ must confront her affinity to both generations as a route to accepting her own situation; her development involves the resolution of conflicting attitudes towards language, the outside world, and the traditional concept of woman.

—Mason Harris, "Broken Generations in *Obasan*: Inner Conflict and the Destruction of Community," *Canadian Literature* 127 (Winter 1990): 41–42

SHIRLEY GEOK-LIN LIM

In works by Japanese American women, such as ⟨Monica Sone's⟩ *Nisei Daughter* and ⟨Joy Kogawa's⟩ *Obasan*, engendered by, complicating and deepening the daughter's bond with and break from the maternal origin, the essential thematics of maternality is also the story of race. In these life stories, the Japanese mother is the figure not only of maternality but also of racial consciousness. The daughters' struggles to separate from their racial origin or to recover it, given the historical context of Japanese American internment, are therefore matters of political as well as psychological urgency. Thus, although such texts force masculinist Asian American critics to come to terms with the significance of women's experience and language in women's writing, they also ask feminist critics to expand their paradigms to include the problematics of race.

Nisei Daughter and *Obasan*, the first presented as autobiography, the second as fiction, are biographically and thematically writings of American daughters born of Asian parents. These two texts illustrate how an initial action—a move to assimilate—is followed by an equal and opposite reaction, a reclamation of the culture of origin. This dialectic, connected to the rejection and reclamation of the mother, in turn entails an attitude toward that American patriarchal system responsible for the internment of Japanese Americans during World War II. The signifying difference between *Nisei Daughter* and *Obasan* lies in the presence of the Japanese mother in the former and the absence of the Japanese mother in the latter. Paradoxically, where the 1953 narrative ⟨*Nisei Daughter*⟩ creates the mother's Japanese presence as a problematic which in the course of political events is repressed and erased, the 1981 narrative presents the Japanese mother's absence as the problematic and the recovery of her lost identity as the means to the daughter's recovery of psychic health. The daughter's quest for the lost mother echoes the "mourning for the mother-daughter relationship" which Cathy N. Davidson and E. M. Broner find in much contemporary women's fiction. ⟨. . .⟩ The reversal of thematics between the two books parallels their generational difference. Just as a too-active Japanese presence during the Pacific War period threatens a generation's attempt to assimilate into a majority white culture, so in a different, postwar generation, one in which political "integration" has been achieved, a lost racial origin may be used to account for and represent feelings of alienation, despair, and psychic deprivation. ⟨. . .⟩

Obasan begins where *Nisei Daughter* ends, with a Japanese Canadian daughter in search of a silenced, lost, and forgotten Japanese mother, and traces the daughter's reconstruction of this absent racial/maternal figure. Countering the repressions of *Nisei Daughter*, *Obasan*, written three decades later, insists on the interrelations between the subject of the "I" and the language through which that subject is expressed and bases the thematics of recuperation of a lost mother in the thematics of the recuperative powers of language itself. In *Obasan*, the writing project is inseparable from the reconstruction of the maternal. The figure of the daughter is also the figure of the writer figuring her self. The images of writer, narrator, speaker, and protagonist collapse into a series of intimately related "I"s ⟨. . . .⟩ *Obasan*, therefore, is both and more than a work of social realism. Using elements from her own life story as well as letters, diaries, and historical documents, Kogawa chose to write a fiction which impersonates the discourse of autobiography while at the same time she has masked the genre of autobiography through the liberating effects of poetic language. The integration of the thematics of the maternal with the text's structure is modernistic and totalizing. The subject of the novel can only be produced in the language of the novel, giving to the work an integrity of depth which distinguishes it from the earlier book.

—Shirley Geok-lin Lim, "Japanese American Women's Life Stories: Maternality in Monica Sone's *Nisei Daughter* and Joy Kogawa's *Obasan*," *Feminist Studies* 16, no. 2 (Summer 1990): 293–94, 301

CHENG LOK CHUA

Much of *Obasan* consists of Naomi's meditative recuperation of her experience of marginality during World War II. And into the texture of Naomi's narrative, Kogawa has woven recurrent leitmotifs, some of the most powerful of which derive from Christian rituals and symbols, specifically Easter, Nebuchadnezzar's fire, Eucharist, and stones into bread; these Christian motifs Kogawa has "displaced" into an ironic narrative mode that makes for a critique of the professed ethics of her structuring majority culture. (In discussion, Kogawa said that she was brought up as a Christian, her father being a pastor and a model for the Reverend Nakayama of *Obasan*; Kogawa also habitually reads a randomly chosen biblical text every morning [Kogawa, tape recording].)

One of the most effective of these Christian symbols is the hoard of toy Easter chicks (67) which Naomi has saved from a previous year's Easter basket. They are intended to be a welcome-back present for her mother when she returns from visiting her dying grandmother in Japan and when she resumes her life in Canada with the new generation. These Christian symbols of new life become ironic because Naomi's Canadian-born mother never does return. Instead, she suffers the horrors of radiation sickness after the bombing of Nagasaki and then is prevented by Canadian authorities from returning to her native land because she has adopted an orphaned niece, also a radiation victim. This ironic reversal negating the hope and rebirth symbolized by these Easter chicks is further heightened by a childhood incident during which Naomi innocently puts some newly bought live Easter chicks into the compound of a mother hen in the belief that the hen would nurture the life of the chicks. Contrary to Naomi's naive expectations, however, the mother hen pecks at the chicks and kills them (58); Kogawa's ironic comment upon the treatment of Japanese by Caucasian Canadians in their own homeland is clear when one notices that the chicks are yellow and the mother hen is white (58).

Kogawa extends this symbol that ought to mean life but that has been ironically displaced into a symbol of death when she imagistically suggests a further breakdown in community relationships in Naomi's nightmares; during her ghost-town years, Naomi is haunted and repulsed by the recollection of an incident in which Japanese boys performed a ritualized killing of a white chicken (154–58). This is certainly a frightening image of hate and reprisal taking precedence over what ought to be love and rebirth in social relationships and rituals.

—Cheng Lok Chua, "Witnessing the Japanese Canadian Experience in World War II: Processual Structure, Symbolism, and Irony in Joy Kogawa's *Obasan*," *Reading the Literatures of Asian America*, ed. Shirley Geok-lin Lim and Amy Ling (Philadelphia: Temple University Press, 1992), 101–2

KING-KOK CHEUNG

By tracing the decline of Naomi's family, Kogawa, like 〈Hisaye〉 Yamamoto and 〈Maxine Hong〉 Kingston, furnishes insights into the matrix of gender and race that go beyond the obvious double jeopardy of minority women and the general equation of men with powerful patriarchs. Japanese Canadian men, too, are emphatically not immune to persecution in *Obasan*. Naomi's grandfather, father, and surrogate father are subject not only to the "Laws of the [white] Ruling Fathers" but also to the "ill-will" of the Canadian Imperial Order of Daughters of the Empire, who, Emily reports, "said we were all spies and saboteurs" (82). The three nikkei fathers are singled out for "special" treatment: they are abruptly separated from their families and put to work in road camps or imprisoned. Stephen, a child at the time of the war, sustains permanent, if invisible, damage: he turns his back on Japanese culture completely.

The silencing inflicted upon each of the male characters constitutes a muted yet distinctive strain in a novel concerned largely with female interaction. ⟨. . .⟩

The experiences of Uncle, Father, and Stephen undermine the popular feminist opposition of powerful males and powerless females. In *Obasan*, as in "The Legend" and *China Men*, racial abuse is as stifling as sexual molestation. The similarity of these two forms of oppression is made explicit by Naomi. When Stephen is beaten up by white boys, he refuses to tell Naomi what has caused his injury. Naomi intuits, "Is he ashamed, as I was in Old Man Gower's bathroom?" (70). Rape, Erika Gottlieb points out, is used here as a "metaphor for any kind of violation." Like Stephen, many Japanese Canadians refuse to describe what Rose calls their "political and spiritual rape" by the Canadian government.

The metaphor effectively secures the connection between oppression and repression. Instead of voicing anger at the subjugators, most victims of rape seal their lips in shame. The child Naomi, whose relationship with her mother has been one of mutual trust, begins to nurse a secret that separates her from her mother after her molestation. Dispossessed and dispersed all over the country after the war, many nikkei tried to assimilate quickly into the dominant culture so as not to be noticed. "None of my friends today are Japanese Canadians," Naomi discloses (38). All she wants at first is to forget the past: "Crimes of history . . . can stay in history. . . . Questions from all these papers, questions referring to turbulence in the past, are an unnecessary upheaval" (41, 45). Her resignation is ultimately complicit with social amnesia: her self-imposed silence feeds the one imposed externally.

—King-Kok Cheung, *Articulate Silences: Hisaye Yamamoto, Maxine Hong Kingston, Joy Kogawa* (Ithaca, NY: Cornell University Press, 1993), 140, 142–43

HEATHER ZWICKER

The problem Kogawa addresses is, how do you make a country your own when it disowns you?

There is no simple answer. In fact, the novel ⟨*Obasan*⟩ exemplifies what ⟨Biddy⟩ Martin and ⟨Chandra Talpade⟩ Mohanty call "the tension between the desire for home, for synchrony, for sameness, and the realization of the repressions and violence that make home, harmony, sameness imaginable, and that enforce it" ⟨"Feminist Politics: What's Home Got to Do with It?" 1986, 208⟩. On the one hand, Naomi has violent dreams of dismemberment: of her legs being sawed in half, of being chased by superhuman beings with hinged metal arms, and, always, of soldiers—the most direct manifestation of the national state apparatus. On the other hand, these dreams take place against the backdrop of Canadian natality:

> Where do any of us come from in this cold country? Oh Canada,
> whether it is admitted or not, we come from you we come from you.
> From the same soil, the slugs and slime and bogs and twigs and roots.
> We come from the country that plucks its people out like weeds and
> flings them into the roadside. We grow in ditches and sloughs,
> untended and spindly. We erupt in the valleys and mountainsides, in
> small towns and back alleys, sprouting upside-down on the prairies,
> our hair wild as spiders' legs, our feet rooted nowhere. We grow
> where we are not seen, we flourish where we are not heard, the thick
> undergrowth of an unlikely planting. ⟨226⟩

In this passage, Kogawa differentiates home as place—the relentlessly verdant national soil that keeps making Canadians of people—from home as political entity, where the undesirable are weeded out. Occupation alone cannot make a home: those unnamed in the history of a place remain unknown and are consequently mistaken for weeds rather than new strains. Kogawa's metaphor implies an ideal vision of Canada as a garden of many species, all of which deserve to be tended. This pluralist position is reiterated by Rough Lock Bill, a man of unspecified ethnicity who saves Naomi's life, literally and, from an ideological point of view, figuratively (143). He says to the young Naomi, " 'Never met a kid didn't like stories. Red skin, yellow skin, white skin, any skin. . . . Don't make sense, do it, all this fuss about skin?' " (145).

Of course, the fuss isn't just about skin, but about stories—about which history, whose history, is recorded, and how it is used—and this is where the pluralist solution runs into trouble. Pluralist history presupposes that several versions of the past exist, and that minority positions need only to be unveiled and included in order to rectify the discrimination that hides them. This in turn presupposes that history *can* be told, that language is expressive rather than mystifying, and that alternate histories, once told, can be heard.

The novel enters this contentious territory by sustaining a debate between Naomi's two aunts, Emily and Obasan. Naomi herself registers a deep ambivalence, by turns suspicious of Emily's stridency and frustrated with Obasan's silence. Aunt Emily, the academic, articulates the commonsensical pro-history position that talking is good, that it lessens pain and aids healing. Habakkuk 2:2, "Write the vision and make it plain," is her slogan (31). History, according to Aunt Emily, is never singular, neutral, or objective. Says she: " 'There's no strength in seeing all sides unless you can act where real measurable injustice exists.' " (35). Hers is an unarguable position, as far as it goes: if oppression takes the form of exclusion, the appropriate solution is inclusion. But she presupposes that the story of internment can be told and, more problematically, that it can be heard and used to modify conventional histories of Canada.

 —Heather Zwicker, "Canadian Women of Color in the New World Order: Marlene Nourbese Philip, Joy Kogawa, and Beatrice Culleton Fight Their Way Home," *Canadian Women Writing Fiction*, ed. Mickey Pearlman (Jackson, MS: University Press of Mississippi, 1993), 147–49

Teruyo Ueki

Central to ⟨the⟩ scheme of disclosure through withholding is Aunt Emily's package, which lies at the heart of the novel's series of nested riddles. The series begins with two little epigraphs, one a quotation from The Book of Revelations and the other a prose poem, both placed before the first chapter. They arouse in the audience a sense of bewilderment by declaring the existence of a hidden thing; the former talks of the "hidden manna" and the latter "the hidden voice." With the opening of the first chapter, we are faced with Naomi's question to her uncle, asking for an answer to the "hidden reason" ⟨Erika Gottlieb, "The Riddle of Concentric Worlds in *Obasan*," 1986, 36⟩ for their annual visit to the prairie overlooking the coulee. However, this mystery is left unanswered till the end. So are the meanings of the first two riddles, until the story is fully unfolded and their metaphorical implications are detected. Coming into the sixth chapter, we become aware of the existence of Emily's hidden package, which, in addition to Emily's diary, newspaper clippings, and official documents, contains a grey cardboard folder that itself contains two envelopes that further contain the letters telling about the victimization of Naomi's mother under the atomic bomb dropped on Nagasaki. However, this information also remains unintelligible to Naomi as well as to the reader until the end of the novel, because the letters are written in Japanese and Obasan does not translate them for her.

 Erika Gottlieb describes this structure of the novel as "a concentric pattern—container hidden within container within container—creating a sense of mystery and tension" (34), though she mainly refers to the first three riddles (hidden manna, hidden voice, hidden reason) as being associated with a three-dimensional landscape—the revelation as indicating a cosmic world, the poem as Naomi's personal psychological wasteland, and the prairie as the

Canadian natural/political landscape. I agree with Gottlieb that the riddles of these three landscapes are interrelated and that the "concentric structure" of the novel "compels the reader to search for a central meaning at the core of the multilayered texture of Naomi's narrative" (34). However, I would like to refer to the way the riddles are arranged as "the folder structure" ⟨. . . .⟩

The structure of the grey cardboard folder and the structure of the novel correspond to each other in their design. The folder has two flaps with a red circle tab on each of them and is closed with a red string twirled around the tabs as a fastener (45 and 220). The two flaps are analogous to the chapters beginning and ending the novel, both of which are set in the same place—the moonlit prairie overlooking the coulee where Naomi comes with her uncle once every year. The two red tabs of the folder match the two little epigraphs of the novel. Mother's secret is contained within the folder, whereas the secrets of the "hidden manna" and "the hidden voice" are folded within the body of the novel. This folder structure evokes the structure of a Buddhist shrine with its two flapping doors, inside of which Kannon, Goddess of Mercy, is enshrined. In Japan, any door with this type of structure is called "door of '*Kannon-biraki*'," meaning "door opened by Kannon." In view of the role played by Mother, ⟨. . .⟩ the image of Kannon begins to be superimposed upon that of Mother in this hidden shrine behind the flapping doors.

The folder structure signifies the interconnectedness of Mother, Aya Obasan, and Aunt Emily. Naomi's dream in chapter thirty-five suggests how the three women are linked. "Mother stood in the center. In her mouth she held a knotted string stem, like the twine and string of Obasan's ball which she keeps in the pantry. From the stem hung a rose, red as a heart" (227). The string in Mother's mouth connects her to Obasan and in turn to Aunt Emily:

> Obasan . . . is winding the twine from Aunt Emily's package onto a
> twine ball she keeps in the pantry. Obasan never discards anything.
> Besides the twine ball, there's a ball of string . . . (44) ⟨. . .⟩

This tri-female structure is superimposed upon the folder structure. The loving hearts of the two aunts are matched with the two red tabs of the folder and tied by the folder's red string, which is connected to Mother's knotted string threaded out of her mouth holding a red rose like a heart at the end. In this linking, Mother situates herself as a central source of love and guidance. "Do not tell Stephen and Naomi [about my tragedy]" (241) entreated Mother's voice, to which the aunts' hearts responded, and the voice was sealed in the folder. The folder, then, was kept in Emily's package, which was eventually left in Obasan's attic in a long silence of over twenty years.

—Teruyo Ueki, "*Obasan*: Revelations in a Paradoxical Scheme," *MELUS* 18, no. 4 (Winter 1993): 8–11

LINDA HUTCHEON

Itsuka continues the story of Naomi Nakane from *Obasan*, Kogawa's earlier novel, as she leaves the prairie town in which she had grown up and first worked and moves to Toronto in 1976. But the real focus is on the middle years of the 1980s, the years that marked the fight for and successful achievement of Japanese Canadian redress for their treatment at the hands of the federal government during World War II. ⟨. . .⟩

Parallel to the story of anger—of the innumerable battles both with the government and within the Japanese Canadian community itself—runs a story of love, as the gentle, silent, fearful Naomi, a self-defined "old-maid orphan, a barren speck of dust . . . a watcher of other people's children," falls in love with a college chaplain, Cedric, who seems to come to incarnate what is good about multicultural Canada ⟨. . . .⟩

⟨. . .⟩ Kogawa has set herself a difficult problem with her first-person narrator, for Naomi is, by her own admission, "unspeakably boring." But we watch her come to life and love as she realizes that loneliness, solitude, invisibility, and silence can be transmuted into community and communication. The persistent metaphors of flight (associated with love, sexuality, and commitment) and of breath, specifically the "breath of life," trace the changes in Naomi away from the woman who could say of herself: "I've always known that on an emotional quotient chart I'd score somewhere between a cactus and a chimpanzee." Cedric, Emily, her estranged brother Stephen, Obasan, Uncle—all play their roles in this change, but it is through a stylistic transformation on the level of metaphors and of "as if" structures of comparison that the reader is led to feel the change. At the beginning, images (often noticeably odd, even almost inappropriate) proliferate, litter the pages, as Naomi admits: "I can't be direct." In her relationship with Cedric, she trusts touch more than words: "Better the instant language of limbs than the stilted messages we form and reform with the tongue." But with the formal announcement of redress comes a change, a "washing of stains through the speaking of words." Still aware that "speech is a trickster, slipping and sliding away," Naomi trusts instead the piece of paper with which the novel itself ends—the government statement that is both an acknowledgement of wrong and a proclamation of ideals: "As a people, Canadians commit themselves to the creation of a society that ensures equality and justice for all. . . ."

The paradox of a wordsmith who distrusts words—and says so within a novel—is a familiar one, but rarely has it been as moving as here. But, battling with this affective power throughout the novel is an equally strong didactic drive, an almost fierce desire to teach us as much as possible about both the Japanese Canadian past history of repression and its recent history of redress. Naomi's words about Cedric describe herself as well: "He may not look like a professor, but he sounds like one much of the time." The multicultural maga-zine, *Bridge*, for which many of the characters work, offers another space for documentation and instruction, and actual speeches by politicians and other figures are reproduced in the text. History and fiction meet, but do not always merge with ease here; the prose and the passion are also connected, as E. M. Forster wanted them to be, but the seams often show. But the personal warmth, commitment, and generosity that characterize the dedication of the book—to all those people involved in bringing redress—are what make the reader as student, for the most part, happy to listen here to the author as teacher.

    —Linda Hutcheon, "Someday," *Canadian Literature* 136 (Spring 1993): 179, 181

RACHELLE KANEFSKY

Through Naomi's evolving philosophical and political consciousness ⟨in *Obasan* and *Itsuka*⟩, Kogawa demonstrates that the struggle for legitimacy in historical representation takes place not in the deconstruction of truth but in the collective defence of truth. One does not, in other words, impose one's presence on the historical record by obfuscating meaning but by clarifying it. Textual evidence in, and the reception of, both *Obasan* and *Itsuka* reveal that it is unconvincing to argue that history is in any meaningful sense fictional in Kogawa's narratives. In other words, it is difficult to read Kogawa's novels as purely discursive acts that have no base in reality. There is, ultimately, a responsible reading of Kogawa's texts—it is a reading that demands that we recognize, as Naomi finally does, that "It matters to get the facts straight" because "Reconciliation can't begin without mutual recognition of [these] facts" (*Obasan* 183).

There are, undoubtedly, many stories of the experience of internment. And even Aunt Emily recognizes that there is no one story of redress. Rather, "There are as many stories as there are people" (*Itsuka* 247). However, what is clearly conveyed in Kogawa's writing is that the sum of all these stories—including her own—constitutes one reality, a single truth: "During and after World War II, Canadians of Japanese ancestry, the majority of whom were cit-izens, suffered unprecedented actions by the Government of Canada against their community" (formal "Acknowledgement," qtd. in Miki and Kobayashi 8; qtd. in *Itsuka* 289). ⟨. . .⟩

⟨. . .⟩ Clearly, in a world in which Nazism is resurfacing as surely as its vic-tims, and their stories, are dying, it is our responsibility to reembrace an epis-temological model that emphasizes belief and meaning. It is only through concrete, rational knowledge, and not through systems of ambiguity and distortion, that the horrors of history can be prevented from reoccurring. It is in this way that "The past," as Kogawa teaches us, "is the future" (*Obasan* 42).

—Rachelle Kanefsky, "Debunking a Postmodern Conception of History: A Defense of Humanist Values in the Novels of Joy Kogawa," *Canadian Literature* 148 (Spring 1996): 29–31

BIBLIOGRAPHY

The Splintered Moon. 1967.
A Choice of Dreams. 1974.
Jericho Road. 1977.
Obasan. 1981.
Woman in the Woods. 1985.
Naomi's Road. 1986.
Itsuka. 1992.

Bharati Mukherjee

b. 1938

BHARATI MUKHERJEE was born in 1938 in Calcutta, India, to an upper-class Hindu family of Brahmin caste, the top of India's social hierarchy. Her parents sent Mukherjee and her sisters to a British convent school and later to private schools in London and Switzerland. Caught, on one hand, between the privileges of caste status and the submissiveness demanded of Indian women and, on the other, between an Indian heritage and an Anglophilic upbringing, Mukherjee experienced a dichotomous childhood. Her allegiance to her native country was weakened by the message ingrained in her by school, family, and community: that the future lay in the West. So, in 1961, she arrived in Iowa City, with a scholarship to attend the writer's workshop at the University of Iowa; she earned an M.F.A. in creative writing and a Ph.D. in English and comparative literature. Her first novel, *The Tiger's Daughter*, explored aspects of the divided allegiance of her childhood.

At the University of Iowa, Mukherjee met and married Clark Blaise; upon graduation, the couple moved to his native Canada. With their two young sons, they first resided in Toronto and later moved to Montreal, where both had teaching positions (at McGill University and Concordia University). However, Canada did not embrace Mukherjee; she experienced overt discrimination, and her writing was largely ignored. Her powerful essay, "An Invisible Woman," and several early short stories reflect her unhappiness during this period and protest the prejudice against Canadians of Indian descent.

Days and Nights in Calcutta and *The Sorrow and the Terror: The Haunting Legacy of the Air India Tragedy*, nonfiction works cowritten by Mukherjee and her husband, consider conflicts between the Third World and the First World, the ordeal of exile, and the immigrant's search for a sense of rootedness. In *Days and Nights*, husband and wife recount, each in a distinct narrative, a year-long visit to Calcutta, creating at once a dual travel memoir and an intimate, self-reflexive look at how each experiences cultural differences. Their second collaboration, *The Sorrow and the Terror*, is an exposé of the crash of Air India Flight 182 that investigates the Canadian government's ineffectual treatment of what was officially declared a "disaster imported from India."

Discouraged by their experiences in Canada, Mukherjee and Blaise finally gave up their tenured professorships in 1980 and moved to the United States. Life in the United States spurred an explosion of creativity for Mukherjee. As a writer-in-residence at Emory University, she finished the short stories for *Darkness*, a disconcerting collection that twists classic diasporic themes into emotional tales of Indian and Pakistani immigrants, stocked with history and fantasy, sex and violence. The couple then made a move that Mukherjee felt was inevitable, to New York City. There she wrote her second collection of short stories, *The Middleman and Other Stories*, which won the 1988 National Book Critics Circle Award for fiction and subsequently sparked interest in her earlier works, expanding her audience in the United States, Europe, and India.

Jasmine, a character from a story that appeared in *The Middleman and Other Stories*, became the central figure in Mukherjee's next novel, *Jasmine*. Named Jyoti upon her birth in India, called Jasmine by the man she married at 14, the heroine of this novel travels to the United States, where she eventually sheds her ethnicity by appropriating the name Jane. The character encapsulates the transformative effect of assimilation, both on newcomers themselves and on American society.

Mukherjee's story "The Tenant" was included in *The Best American Short Stories of 1987*, and a screenplay for *Days and Nights in Calcutta* is being developed. She has received grants from the National Endowment for the Arts and the Guggenheim Foundation and lives in Manhattan, where she teaches creative writing at Columbia University and Queens College.

CRITICAL EXTRACTS

ROBERT S. ANDERSON

⟨. . .⟩ Clark Blaise and Bharati Mukherjee have written a kind of travel memoir ⟨*Days and Nights*⟩, in which they want to understand their attraction to Calcutta. ⟨. . .⟩

⟨. . .⟩ It is ambitious because two writers of different styles and background try to capture the complexity of their involvement with disparate aspects of life in India. The larger contribution is from Clark but Bharati's is better written and better pruned, and to me, more interesting. It is an intimate book because these two writers are also married to each other, and each describes what the other is experiencing; there are spousely asides about the other's reactions, moods, preconceptions, or cultural background. ⟨. . .⟩

The book is organized in two parts, and each writer has an epilogue. This duality offered opportunities for fine counterpoint writing, but the work is not disciplined in that manner. Occasionally an event like a wedding or film premiere is reported by both Clark and Bharati. We can thus anticipate the potential of the Rashomon-effect if it were employed consistently: it would confer on the text the fullest advantages of their two quite different perspectives and experience. Meanwhile they are also re-examining their own relationships; Bharati is able to see Clark in an environment unfamiliar to him but familiar to her, while Clark tries to separate his relationship to Bharati and to India (which would at least amuse linguists, as Bharat is the Sanscrit name for much of what is now India).

There is much reflection on epistemological questions—on how one knows India, how one discovers the truth, and what stance should be taken as writer towards "facts" or "India," or towards one's audience. Clark's project is quite clear:

> What is the "real" Bombay, the real India, the real anything for a fiction writer? ⟨. . .⟩

Bharati's project is just as ambitious and complex, but more self-reflexive. She re-explores the networks of her family, and reflects on her childhood and schooling ("the geometry of one's birth") while meeting wealthy former classmates or film makers like Satyajit Ray. She is as much concerned with a stance to take as with modes of discovery. Confirming there is such a thing as the Hindu imagination, she sees it in "the inspired and crazy vision" of a sculptured frieze of a temple, marking "the enormity of detail. Nothing has been excluded." The message of this vision is "merge—there are no insides and outsides, no serpents, no gods." In contrast to "traditional" India, "where metaphor and reality continually change places," she says "we have confined ourselves to single obsessions."

—Robert S. Anderson, "Calcutta Chronicle," *Canadian Literature* 76 (Spring 1978): 111–12

Mahnaz Ispahani

In the introduction to Bharati Mukherjee's first collection of short stories, she makes the interesting observation that the book she dreams of updating is no longer *A Passage to India* ⟨E. M. Forster⟩, but *Call it Sleep* ⟨Henry Roth⟩. The stories that follow do indeed treat the classical theme of diaspora—of exile and emigration, of all the acts of courage and will required by the experience, all the traumas and ironies and failures of it. But Mukherjee's diaspora will not be completely familiar to most readers. This is Henry Roth with a subcontinental twist.

Some of the finest writing in England in recent years has been fiction by or about immigrants from the subcontinent. In America, where there is a substantial community of such people, there has been far less interest in them. ⟨The prose of Bharati Mukherjee may help to remedy this situation.⟩ Her stories are populated by Indian and Pakistani immigrants, new inhabitants of a tense, hostile Canada and a flat, urgent America. Her people rarely lose sight of what she calls, very rightly, their "not-quiteness." They bring with them the psychic extremes and historical turmoil of India's present and past. They crave success and stability in their adopted homes, yet are torn by the consequences of their new identities. The discomfiting tales in *Darkness* are about building new lives with old materials; their settings may seem simple, but the emotional landscape they describe is not.

Mukherjee writes in many voices. She is a child, a young woman, an old man; a Moslem, a Hindu, a Sikh; a rich doctor, an illegal waiter. She comes from India, from Pakistan, from Bangladesh. She observes the immigrant family struggling to overcome racism and the other forms of social distance, while trying at the same time to work out compromises between the powerful traditional culture of its origins and the mores of its new home. The compromises are not always successful; and so her stories almost always seem to turn on misunderstandings and mistaken assumptions, on confused attempts to cope, on chaotic and often brutal responses. Mukherjee's work is riddled with mixed affairs and mixed marriages that don't exactly work, with unions arranged in India that are stretched to the seams in America, with the confused children of such unions. And the children, in her account, seem doubly lost, pulled between a strong magical past that they have themselves barely known and the strange, seductive reality of America.

—Mahnaz Ispahani, "A Passage from India," *The New Republic* (14 April 1986): 36

POLLY SHULMAN

In Bharati Mukherjee's fiction, sex and violence circle each other like twin stars. At best they're universal languages, ways to communicate across cultural walls. At worst, they're gestures that can't be ignored, even when they're not understood. Her subject is the sparks that happen when cultures meet. With rapes and riots, suttee and tender acts of adultery, her characters try to talk to each other in languages they've half forgotten or never completely learned. ⟨. . .⟩

Taking V. S. Naipaul as a model, she wrote with self-protective irony, particularly apparent in her second novel, *Wife* (1975). Dimple Basu, the heroine, is an exile in New York, the bride in a traditional arranged marriage; she's one of the characters for whom double vision means a divided self. Slowly Dimple cracks up, and the book ends in an act of not very convincing violence—

Mukherjee keeps Dimple and her world at arm's length. But after moving to the U.S. Mukherjee underwent a transformation. Seeing herself in the tradition of Ellis Island American writers—*Darkness* is dedicated to Bernard Malamud—she shed "the aloofness of expatriation" for "the exuberance of immigration."

The change came upon her suddenly, she says, and it's easy to pick out the earlier stories in *Darkness*. "Hindus" and "The World According to Hsu" seem diffuse, full of frustrated anger. "Isolated Incidents," about Paki-bashing in Toronto, is almost pedantic; like one of her own middlemen, Mukherjee is addressing people she knows aren't listening, so she has to shout a little to be heard. The newer stories, though, make up for these lapses. "Angela," "A Father," "Saints," and just about all the stories in *The Middleman* are as subtle as *The Tiger's Daughter*, and even sharper—either Mukherjee is now confident that she can interpret to her new countrymen, or she's writing for herself. ⟨. . .⟩

Immigration for Mukherjee needn't mean assimilation. The melting pot, yes, but it's the lumps that interest her. Assimilation implies forgetting, blotting out the past, but this past is what the present is made of. If she weren't still an Indian, Mukherjee wouldn't be the wonderful American writer she is.

—Polly Shulman, "Home Truths: Bharati Mukherjee, World Citizen," *Voice Literary Supplement* 66 (June 1988): 19

JONATHAN RABAN

When Bharati Mukherjee dedicated her last collection of stories about immigrants, "Darkness," to Bernard Malamud, she was both saluting an old friend and bedding herself down in a tradition. In modern American fiction, the immigrant has classically been Jewish: Jewish writers, from Abraham Cahan through Henry Roth to Malamud himself, have reworked the facts of their history into a rich body of literary mythology. In "Darkness," Ms. Mukherjee (who was brought up in Calcutta, lived in Canada, has a doctorate from the University of Iowa and has written two novels as well as short stories) successfully grafted her own experience as an Indian on to that of the American Jews. Now, in "The Middleman," she hijacks the whole tradition of Jewish American writing and flies it off to a destination undreamed of by its original practitioners.

Her characters have a great deal in common with their Jewish counterparts: they're heroes to themselves, a size larger than life, and they see the surfaces of America with the bug-eyed hangover clarity of the greenhorn afloat in a gaudy new world. Yet they're not tired, huddled or even poor: they own motels, work scams, teach in college, breeze through on private funds. Their diaspora is a haphazard, pepperpot dispersal. They have been shaken out, singly, over a huge territory, from Toronto in the north down to a steamy Central American republic. They're in Ann Arbor, Cedar Falls, Rock Springs,

Flushing, Manhattan, suburban New Jersey, Atlanta, Florida. With no Lower East Side to keep the manners and morals of the old world alive, they're on their own and on the make. How the introspective and overmothered sons of the ghetto, from David Levinsky to Alexander Portnoy, would have envied Ms. Mukherjee's new Americans—their guiltlessness, bounce, sexual freedom, their easy money and the lightness of their footsteps on the American land-scape. Unlike their Jewish literary ancestors, Ms. Mukherjee's people are no more tormented by conscience than butterflies.

The stories in "The Middleman" are streets ahead of those in "Darkness," fine as that collection was. Not only has Ms. Mukherjee vastly enlarged her geographical and social range (the immigrants in her new book come fresh to America from Vietnam, the Caribbean, the Levant, Afghanistan, the Philippines, Italy and Sri Lanka, as well as from India), but she has greatly sharpened her style. Her writing here is far quicker in tempo, more confident and more sly than it used to be. There's no slack in it, as there was in some of the "Darkness" stories, and no Creative Writing. It's so tight and so packed with internal references that it's hard to quote ⟨. . . .⟩

Most of the stories are monologues, spoken by compulsively fluent talk-ers whose lives are too urgent and mobile for them to indulge in the luxury of the retrospective past tense. They hit the page in full flight, and they move through the stories as they move through the world, at speed, with the reader straining to keep up with them. Throughout the book, the idiom of America in the 1980's is handled by Ms. Mukherjee with much the same rapturous affection and acuteness of ear that Nabokov, another immigrant, brought to the idiom of America in the 1950's in "Lolita." On one level, "The Middleman" is a consummated romance with the American language.

—Jonathan Raban, "Savage Boulevards, Easy Streets," *The New York Times Book Review* (19 June 1988): 1, 22

ALISON B. CARB

Carb: Do you see changes in your writing style in *The Middleman?*

Mukherjee: My style has changed because I am becoming more Americanized with each passing year. American fiction has a kind of energy that fiction from other cultures seems to lack right now. The stories in *The Middleman,* I like to think, have this energy and passion as well. Each character and story suggests a different style.

When I sit down in my study to write, I don't immediately say, "I have to write an experimental story." The story idea itself dictates the appropriate voice for it and how lean or fleshy a paragraph might be. I write some stories from a very authoritative third person point of view. With others I use an inti-mate, textured style and a first person point of view.

My first novel, *The Tiger's Daughter,* has a rather British feel to it. I used the omniscient point of view and plenty of irony. This was because my concept of language and notions of how a novel was constructed were based on British models. I had gone to school in London as a young child and later to a British convent school for elite young women in post-colonial India, where we read English writers like Jane Austen and E. M. Forster.

By the time I wrote *Darkness* I had adopted American English as my language. I moved away from using irony and was no longer comfortable using an authoritative point of view. In addition, I started to write short stories instead of novels. The short story form requires us to express our thoughts concisely and not waste a single sentence or detail.

Carb: How does your writing contrast with that of other India-born writers?

Mukherjee: There is a large difference between myself and these authors. Unlike writers such as Anita Desai and R. K. Narayan, I do not write in Indian English about Indians living in India. My role models, view of the world, and experiences are unlike theirs. These writers live in a world in which there are still certainties and rules. They are part of their society's mainstream. Wonderful writers as they are, I am unable to identify with them because they describe characters who fit into their community in different ways than my naturalized Americans fit into communities in Queens or Atlanta.

On the other hand, I don't write from the point of an Indian expatriate like V. S. Naipaul. Naipaul, who was born in Trinidad because his relatives left India involuntarily to settle there, has different attitudes about himself. He writes about living in perpetual exile and about the impossibility of ever having a home. Like Naipaul, I am a writer from the Third World but unlike him I left India by choice to settle in the U.S. I have adopted this country as my home. I view myself as an American author in the tradition of other American authors whose ancestors arrived at Ellis Island.

—Alison B. Carb, "An Interview with Bharati Mukherjee," *The Massachusetts Review* (Winter 1988/89): 649–50

MICHAEL GORRA

Bharati Mukherjee's third novel ⟨Jasmine⟩ carries the same title as one of the best stories in her prize-winning collection of last year, "The Middleman and Other Stories." ⟨. . .⟩

For the rich novel that's grown from that story, Ms. Mukherjee has shifted the narrative into the first person and placed her heroine's origins in the Punjab rather than Trinidad, where the added weight of tradition makes the character's love affair with the possibilities of America all the more exhilarating. "Lifetimes ago," the novel begins, "under a banyan tree in the village of Hasnapur, an astrologer cupped his ears—his satellite dish to the stars—and foretold my widowhood and exile." But the 7-year-old Jyoti—not yet Jasmine, still less the Jane she'll become when she invents a new life in Iowa—rejects the fate he assigns her. Which of them is right? ⟨. . .⟩

Reading Ms. Mukherjee's short stories about immigrants, I've often thought of the Irish writer Frank O'Connor's argument that while the novel deals with the structure of society, the short story tends to concentrate on what he calls "the lonely voice," on "outlawed figures wandering about" on that society's fringes. In expanding that sense of marginality into the material of a novel, Ms. Mukherjee has made her heroine emblematic of this nation of outsiders as a whole, but she's done so without losing a short story's virtues, above all its sense of speed and compression, its sense of a life distilled into its essence.

"Jasmine" is so tightly made one wants to read it in a sitting. Yet, paradoxically, that's also the novel's chief weakness. Its other characters, however vivid, remain too firmly subordinated to Jasmine. Their stories matter only insofar as they affect hers, in a way that not only suggests the novel's origins as a short story, but that troubles me precisely because those characters are so vivid. It's not easy, as Jasmine lights out for the territories once more, to view her abandonment of Jane Ripplemeyer's responsibilities with the complacency the novel seems to call for. Yet perhaps that uneasiness is intended; perhaps "Jasmine" is as much an implicit criticism of the self-absorption of American life as it is a celebration of its inventive openness.

What does seem clear is that Ms. Mukherjee wants the question posed by the astrologer's prediction to remain an open one. Jasmine may in some ways be in control of her own destiny, but she is also a widow and in exile. Or rather in an exile that she chooses to redefine as immigration—as the Indian-born Ms. Mukherjee herself has recently done in choosing to become an American citizen. As a young writer, Ms. Mukherjee has said, she dreamed of updating "A Passage to India"; now, she writes, it's Henry Roth's immigrant classic "Call It Sleep." "Jasmine" stands as one of the most suggestive novels we have about what it is to become an American.

—Michael Gorra, "Call It Exile, Call It Immigration," *The New York Times Book Review* (10 September 1989): 9

BHARATI MUKHERJEE

⟨My⟩ literary agenda begins by acknowledging that America has transformed *me*. It does not end until I show how I (and the hundreds of thousands like me) have transformed America.

The agenda is simply stated, but in the long run revolutionary. Make the familiar exotic; the exotic familiar.

I have had to create an audience. I cannot rely on shorthand references to my community, my religion, my class, my region, or my old school tie. I've had to sensitize editors as well as readers to the richness of the lives I'm writing about. The most moving form of praise I receive from readers can be summed up in three words: *I never knew.* Meaning, I see these people (call them Indians, Filipinos, Koreans, Chinese) around me all the time and I never knew they had an inner life. I never knew they schemed and cheated, suffered, felt so strongly, cared so passionately. When even the forms of praise are so rudimentary, the writer knows she has an inexhaustible fictional population to enumerate. Perhaps even a mission, to appropriate a good colonial word.

I have been blessed with an enormity of material. I can be Chekhovian and Tolstoyan—with melancholy and philosophical perspectives on the breaking of hearts as well as the fall of civilizations—and I can be a brash and raucous homesteader, Huck Finn and Woman Warrior, on the unclaimed plains of American literature. My material, reduced to jacket-flap copy, is the rapid and dramatic transformation of the United States since the early 1970s. Within that perceived perimeter, however, I hope to wring surprises.

Yet (I am a writer much given to "yet") my imaginative home is also in the tales told by my mother and grandmother, the world of the Hindu epics. For all the hope and energy I have placed in the process of immigration and accommodation—I'm a person who couldn't ride a public bus when she first arrived, and now I'm someone who watches tractor pulls on obscure cable channels—there are parts of me that remain Indian, parts that slide against the masks of newer selves. The form that my stories and novels take inevitably reflects the resources of Indian mythology—shape-changing, miracles, godly perspectives. My characters can, I hope, transcend the straitjacket of simple psychologizing. The people I write about are culturally and politically several hundred years old: consider the history they have witnessed (colonialism, technology, education, liberation, civil war, uprooting). They have shed old identities, taken on new ones, and learned to hide the scars. They may sell you newspapers, or clean your offices at night.

—Bharati Mukherjee, "Four-Hundred-Year-Old Woman," *The Writer on Her Work: New Essays in New Territory*, vol. 2, ed. Janet Sternburg (New York: W. W. Norton & Company, Inc., 1991), 35–36

Arvindra Sant-Wade and Karen Marguerite Radell

The female protagonist in one of Bharati Mukherjee's prize-winning short stories, from the collection titled *The Middleman and Other Stories*, is shocked when her landlord lover refers to the two of them as "two wounded people," and thinks to herself that "She knows she is strange, and lonely, but being Indian is not the same, she would have thought, as being a freak" (113). The Indian woman, Maya Sanyal, who is the central figure of the story, "The Tenant," recognizes her strangeness in America and her appalling loneliness, but she resists being recognized as a "freak." No doubt this term occurs to her when her current lover, Fred, a man without arms, refers to them both as wounded. She does not see herself as being as freakish as Fred, as bereft as Fred, though certainly the story makes clear that she has been wounded emotionally and spiritually by the struggle to come to terms with her new life in America. In one sense, Fred's assessment is accurate, for as the author indicates in all the stories in this collection, it is impossible to adapt to life in the New World without sustaining some kind of wound to one's spirit.

It is apparently a deeper wound for the women of the Third World, who are engaged in the struggle to fashion a new identity for themselves in an alien culture. Perhaps this struggle results from their sudden freedom from the bonds of superstition and chauvinism that held them fast in their old, familiar cultures, freedom that seems to leave them floating, unbalanced, in the complex, sometimes treacherous air of this new and unfamiliar culture. The irony is that this refashioning of the self is both painful and exhilarating; hence, the terrible ambivalence of the women toward their own freedom—the freedom to *become*—an ambivalence expressed by these women in the midst of arduous change, in the powerful act of rejecting the past and moving energetically toward an unknown future. ⟨. . .⟩

⟨. . .⟩ Her characters, she asserts, "are filled with a hustlerish kind of energy" and, more importantly,

> they take risks they wouldn't have taken in their old, comfortable worlds to solve their problems. As they change citizenship, they are reborn. ⟨Alison Carb, "An Interview with Bharati Mukherjee," 1988, 654⟩

Mukherjee's choice of metaphor is especially apt with reference to the women in her fiction, for the act of rebirth, like birth itself, is both painful, and, after a certain point, inevitable. It is both terrible and wonderful, and an act or process impossible to judge while one is in the midst of it. So the women in Mukherjee's stories are seen deep in this process of being reborn, of refashioning themselves, so deep that they can neither extricate themselves nor reverse the process, nor, once it has begun, would they wish to. There is a part of themselves, however, that is able to stand back a little and observe their own reaction to the process, their own ambivalence. We know this because Mukherjee weaves contradiction into the very fabric of the stories: positive assertions in interior monologues are undermined by negative visual images; the liberation of change is undermined by confusion or loss of identity; beauty is undermined by sadness.

> —Arvindra Sant-Wade and Karen Marguerite Radell, "Refashioning the Self: Immigrant Women in Bharati Mukherjee's New World," *Studies in Short Fiction* 29, no. 1 (Winter 1992): 11–12

CRAIG TAPPING

A major theme in Mukherjee's nonfiction is that Indians in Canada have been subjected to racist assaults, physically and psychologically. The government has failed its citizens. She writes that she identifies with these victims, and she has explained her own traumatic sense of entrapment and claustrophobia while living in Canada ("Invisible Woman"). The claims of identification are frequently couched in terms of class expectation, without apology: "Great privilege had been conferred upon me; my struggle was to work hard enough to deserve it. And I did. This bred confidence, but not conceit. . . . Calcutta equipped me to survive theft or even assault; it did not equip me to accept proof of my unworthiness" ("Invisible Woman" 36, 38). Even in the recent essay on Rushdie, Mukherjee does not demur from such contextualizing. This is the generation who "traded top-dog status in the homeland for the loss-of-face meltdown of immigration" ("Prophet and Loss" 12). Unfortunately, this knowledge of the life, foregrounded by the essayist in her readers' consciousnesses, limits the ability of some North American critics—with their almost endemic but often vicarious interest in politically correct and socially austere lives—to read the fictions sensibly.

  If she is right that she wants to embrace the new, the dilemma is that she also carries a lot of the old with her—which we then read as élitism and class-exclusive aspirations. Rejection on these grounds, however, suggests that only those who have suffered or continue to suffer explicit economic violence should testify against a bourgeois culture's insensitivities. These "others" have no voice or access to that discourse in the first place. Thus, in both instances, we use such rules to silence a community.

> —Craig Tapping, "South Asia Writes North America: Prose Fictions and Autobiographies from the Indian Diaspora," *Reading the Literatures of Asian America,* ed. Shirley Geok-lin Lim and Amy Ling (Philadelphia: Temple University Press, 1992), 294–95

GARY BOIRE

Jasmine is Bharati Mukherjee's first novel in fourteen years; like her stories, it is highly crafted, impeccably understated, and virtually seamless in its unfolding.

It is also, like many of her public statements and much of her writing, controversial. Like ⟨Margaret⟩ Atwood, Mukherjee has attracted a network of hecklers who pay more attention to her biography than her texts, and who delight in gainsaying as self-promotional Mukherjee's many observations about exclusionary racism and the Canadian literary scene. In this "word of mouth" category *Jasmine* has already gathered clusters of disagreeing admirers and critics. What for one reader is a startlingly intense "de-Europeanization" of the western/American novel (a hybrid mixture of romance, murder, and travel genres), is for another an opportunistic ride on the currently faddish postcolonial bandwagon. Just another novel about emigration, cultural difference, language, and racism. I mention this kind of extraneous networking because it is, to my mind, precisely the kind of detrimental gossip that would distort and ultimately disguise what I think is a very impressive and very important novel. *Jasmine* is a deceptively simple allegory which deliberately sabotages through rewriting. ⟨. . .⟩

In one sense, this story tells *the* paradigmatic "postcolonial" narrative: it is *the* story that "tells" Euro- and Americocentricity back into itself by reversing readerly (read Anglo-American) expectations, by including all that is usually excluded, by bringing inside what is usually left outside. Mukherjee's crippled American banker who falls in love with a Punjabi woman and who then adopts a Vietnamese son (both of whom, interestingly, leave him to "rebirth" elsewhere and with others) develops into a resistant allegory that deconstructs the allure of American mythology. Horatio Alger may whisper from the wings, but he never steals the show. In fact, he is banished in short order.

But *Jasmine* is a "retelling" of considerably greater sophistication than ⟨a⟩ mere plot summary would indicate. Mukherjee writes with an almost surgical sense of irony (and indeed there is relatively little back-thumping humour to be found), an irony that subtly dismantles/unravels a history of oppressive positionings. ⟨. . .⟩

Jasmine is a tremendously interesting work, not simply because it foregrounds characters and situations and nationalities so often disguised or dismissed in the western/American tradition, but primarily because of Mukherjee's ironic nuance and sinewy revisionism. This is an important book not only for what it says, but also for how it says it. Mukherjee's is a revisionary, appropriative technique, one that "channels" deeply (to borrow from one of her rare comic scenes) into an existent literary landscape in order to excavate her own highly deserved space.

—Gary Boire, "Eyre & Anglos," *Canadian Literature* 132 (Spring 1992): 160–61

B I B L I O G R A P H Y

The Tiger's Daughter. 1972.

Wife. 1975.

Days and Nights in Calcutta (with Clark Blaise). 1977.

The Sorrow and the Terror: The Haunting Legacy of the Air India Tragedy (with Clark Blaise). 1985.

Darkness. 1985.

The Middleman and Other Stories. 1988.

Jasmine. 1990.

Amy Tan

b. 1952

AMY TAN was born in Oakland, California, on February 19, 1952, to John and Daisy Tan, both first-generation Chinese immigrants. Her father, a minister and electrical engineer, and her mother, a vocational nurse, were forced to leave behind three other daughters in China when they emigrated to the United States. The eruption of the Communist Revolution destroyed not only all hope of sending for the girls but also any means of contact with them. Between Tan's 15th and 16th birthdays, the family's burden of loss intensified with the deaths of both her older brother and her father from brain tumors. Her mother fled from the site of this emotional devastation to Switzerland with her remaining children. This grief, experienced so early in life, later becomes a recurring element in Tan's novels.

Returning to the United States as a young woman, Tan earned bachelor's and master's degrees in English and linguistics at San Jose State University, where she also met her future husband, Lou DeMattei. In 1976, she dropped out of the Ph.D. program at the University of California, Berkeley, devastated by the murder of a close friend. For the next three years, she worked as a language specialist with disabled children and as a freelance medical and technical writer. An admitted workaholic, Tan joined the Squaw Valley Community of Writers with the simple intention of developing a hobby, but out of her early efforts grew her first novel, *The Joy Luck Club*.

Published in 1989, *The Joy Luck Club* was enthusiastically recieved by critics and the public. Autobiographical strands are woven throughout the text, in which interlocking vignettes portray the generational and cultural differences between American-born daughters and their Chinese-born mothers. Though Tan was criticized by some for co-opting Chinese-American culture, most critics professed her uncommon command of language and storytelling a rarity among first-time authors. *The Joy Luck Club* landed on the *New York Times* best-seller list for nine months, and then Hollywood brought the story to an even larger audience. Produced by Oliver Stone, directed by Wayne Wang, and with a screenplay cowritten by Tan, the film version was both a critical and commercial achievement and notable for its Asian and Asian-American cast.

In 1991, Tan published her second novel, *The Kitchen God's Wife*, a gripping, bittersweet story about a young woman searching for greater understanding of her Chinese mother's background. The novel was again both a critical and popular success, and many reviewers exclaimed that Tan had not only met but exceeded expectations raised by her first book. Tan's first two books have since been translated into more than 20 languages.

Tan's latest novel, *The Hundred Secret Senses*, follows the lives of two sisters, American-born Olivia Yee and her Chinese half-sister, Kwan, who is brought to the United States to fulfill their father's deathbed request. Although Tan experiments with magic realism, her signature narrative scheme and themes of generational and cultural conflict are perhaps too familiar a configuration; many reviewers found the book unsatisfying and less well constructed and convincing than her previous works.

Tan lives with her husband in San Francisco and New York. In addition to her three novels, she has also written two children's books, *The Moon Lady* and *The Chinese Siamese Cat*.

CRITICAL EXTRACTS

ORVILLE SCHELL

Woven into the narrative of the lives of June and her mother are the stories of the three other Joy Luck aunties and their California-born daughters. Moving back and forth across the divide between the two generations, the two continents and the two cultures, we find ourselves transported across the Pacific Ocean from the upwardly mobile, design-conscious, divorce-prone and Americanized world of the daughters in San Francisco to the world of China in the 20's and 30's, which seems more fantastic and dreamlike than real.

We come to see how the idea of China—nourished in America by nothing more than the memories of this vanished reality—has slowly metamorphosed in the minds of the aunties until their imaginations have so overtaken actual memory that revery is all that is left to keep them in contact with the past. When we are suddenly jerked by these sequences from the comforting familiarity of the United States into a scared child's memory of a dying grandmother in remote Ningbo, to remembrances of an arranged marriage with a murderous ending in Shansi or to recollections of a distraught woman abandoning her babies during wartime in Guizhou, we may readily feel bewildered and lost. Such abrupt transitions in time and space make it difficult to know who is who and what the complex web of generational Joy Luck Club relationships actually is.

But these *recherches* to old China are so beautifully written that one should just allow oneself to be borne along as if in a dream. In fact, as the story progresses, the reader begins to appreciate just how these disjunctions work for, rather than against, the novel. While we as readers grope to know whose mother or grandmother is getting married in an unfamiliar ceremony, or why a concubine is committing suicide, we are ironically being reminded not just of the nightmarishness of being a woman in traditional China, but of the enormity of the confusing mental journey Chinese emigrants had to make. And, most ironic, we are also reminded by these literary disjunctions that it is precisely this mental chasm that members of the younger generation must now recross in reverse in order to resolve themselves as whole Chinese-Americans; in "The Joy Luck Club" we get a suggestion of the attendant confusion they must expect to endure in order to get to the other side.

In the hands of a less talented writer such thematic material might easily have become overly didactic, and the characters might have seemed like cutouts from a Chinese-American knockoff of "Roots." But in the hands of Amy Tan, who has a wonderful eye for what is telling, a fine ear for dialogue, a deep empathy for her subject matter and a guilelessly straightforward way of writing, they sing with a rare fidelity and beauty. She has written a jewel of a book.

 —Orville Schell, "Your Mother Is in Your Bones," *The New York Times Book Review* (19 March 1989): 28

DAVID GATES

⟨In *The Joy Luck Club*⟩ Tan lets each woman tell her own story; at the center of every tale is the ferocious love between mother and daughter. ("How can she be her own person?" one mother asks rhetorically. "When did I give her up?") On the periphery are some of the most worthless men this side of "The Color Purple." Such an ambitious narrative scheme would be a handful for any writer; inevitably the voices sound alike, and the ill-chosen menfolk seem interchangeable. So do the mothers' awful life stories. Any of these resilient "aunties" of today could be grafted onto any of those long-suffering girls of wartime China and seem equally plausible.

But Tan is so gifted that none of this matters much. Her eye ranges from the exotic (mountain peaks, like "giant fried fish heads") to the homely (bunk beds with "scuffed, splintery ladders"); she suggests unwritten scenes with a single detail, as in Waverly's reminiscence of her ex-husband with "one hundred forty-six straight black hairs on his chest." Her best device is what Vladimir Nabokov, another chess-obsessed novelist, once characterized as a "knight's move": an oblique change of direction at the end of a passage that suddenly throws everything before it into ironic context. (He was discussing

Jane Austen.) Waverly first plays chess on her brother's set, a hand-me-down from a condescending church lady. "When we got home, my mother told Vincent to throw the chess set away. 'She not want it. We not want it,' she said, tossing her head stiffly to the side with a tight, proud smile." A merely senti-mental writer would stop here; Tan goes on. "My brothers had deaf ears. They were already lining up the chess pieces and reading from the dog-eared instruction book." This is "The Joy Luck Club" at its best: showing the tragi-comic conflicts of cultures and of generations, and never telling a word.

—David Gates, "A Game of Show Not Tell," *Newsweek* (17 April 1989): 68–69

NANCY WILLARD

Through the mothers' stories ⟨in *The Joy Luck Club*⟩ runs a common thread: the fate of the woman who has been taught to efface herself in the name of obe-dience but knows there is something better. "[A] girl should stand still," Ying-Ying St. Clair recalls being told. "If you are still for a very long time, a dragonfly will no longer see you. Then it will come to you and hide in the comfort of the shadow." Lindo Jong, whose disastrous marriage is arranged when she is two, promises herself on the way to the wedding that she will both remember her parents' wishes and keep a sense of who she is. ⟨. . .⟩

For their American daughters, the mothers want nothing less than perfec-tion. They believe that anything is possible for a daughter if the mother wills it. And so the mothers visit on their daughters the sin of demanding perfect obedience. They criticize, manage, manipulate. There are only two kinds of daughters, June's mother tells her. "Those who are obedient and those who fol-low their own mind! Only one kind of daughter can live in this house. Obedient daughter!" In a free society, the daughters are not free to fall short of their mothers' expectations. And so even the most successful daughters are haunted by a sense of failure, and even the most determined mothers are dis-mayed to find their daughters repeating their own weaknesses.

> And even though I taught my daughter the opposite, still she came out the same way! Maybe it is because she was born to me and she was born a girl. And I was born to my mother and I was born a girl. All of us are like stairs, one step after another, going up and down, but all going the same way. (p. 215) ⟨. . .⟩

Amy Tan's special accomplishment in this novel is not her ability to show us how mothers and daughters hurt each other, but how they love and ulti-mately forgive each other. If the book has a plot, it is her characters' slow progress from confusion to understanding. She gives us no easy revelations, only fragile moments of insight and longing. A crushing remark can destroy them. But these moments, as Amy Tan writes them, illuminate that complex relationship for all of us.

—Nancy Willard, "Tiger Spirits," *The Women's Review of Books* 6, nos. 10–11 (July 1989): 12

AMY LING

The stories ⟨in *The Joy Luck Club*⟩ are rich in imagery and sharp detail while the individual personalities (within each generation) are less defined. In fact, in existential fashion, actions and events define and identify the characters, who become who they are because of what they have chosen to do. Thus, though the eight characters are divided into four families and given different names, the book itself is concerned more with a simple bifurcation along generational lines: mothers, whose stories all took place in China, and daughters, whose stories are being lived in America; mothers who are possessively trying to hold fast and daughters who are battling for autonomy. The one story, the Woo's, in which the mother/daughter bond is broken by the mother's death, ceases to be a battle and becomes a devastating loss, a loss compensated for by the daughter's taking the place of the mother and finding mother substitutes. The lost mother is entangled with the story of two lost daughters, who when found and returned to the family become a means of recovering the mother. Further, the lost mother in Jing-mei's story develops into a trope for the lost mother-land for all the daughters.

The four sides of the mahjong table, called "winds" in the game, serve both as a structural and a symbolic device. The novel is divided into four main sections with the focus shifting from one family to the next in each section, allowing mothers and daughters to tell their stories in the first person and making two complete rounds of the table. The exception is Suyuan Woo, who, having recently died, does not speak for herself but whose daughter, Jing-mei, speaks four times, telling her mother's story as she takes her mother's place at the mahjong table and on the fateful trip to China. The symbolic purpose of the cardinal point winds is apparent in Tan's giving a preeminent place to Jing-mei Woo's position at "the East, where things begin" and where the novel begins and ends, making the Woo story central and alluding, of course, to China, where the mothers' lives began.

Further, the winds play a metaphoric role. In mother Lindo Jong's early life, though forced into an arranged marriage, she discovers her own inner strength, and says "I was strong. I was pure . . . I was like the wind" (58). She uses her wind, her breath, to blow out her husband's end of the wedding candle, a courageous act of sabotage that she later makes use of to free herself from this unhappy marriage. Much later in life, she instructs her daughter Waverly on "the art of invisible strength," applicable equally to the game of chess and to life: "Wise guy, he not go against wind. In Chinese we say, Come from South, blow with wind—poom!—North will follow. Strongest wind cannot be seen" (89). In other words, victory over hostile forces (the cold North wind) may be achieved not through direct confrontation but by apparent accommodation and giving in (warm South wind). A simple maneuver in Chinese martial arts illustrates this principle well. If someone of greater weight pushes against you, attempting to knock you over, instead of pushing back you simply step backward, and your opponent, expecting resistance, will be knocked off balance by the force of his own thrust.

Extending the wind imagery in *The Joy Luck Club*, daughter Rose Hsu Jordan says, "I still listened to my mother, but I also learned how to let her words blow through me" (191). And, finally, the balance and imbalance of winds reflects the balance or imbalance in the emotional lives and the power struggles of the characters, most vividly exemplified in the stories of Ying-ying and Lena St. Clair.

Each of the four sections of *The Joy Luck Club* begins with a prologue, a brief narrative, emblematic of that section's theme. The first paragraph of the first prologue contains a rich image that resonates throughout the entire novel:

> The old woman remembered a swan she had bought many years ago
> in Shanghai for a foolish sum. This bird, boasted the market vendor,
> was once a duck that stretched its neck in hopes of becoming a
> goose, and now look!—it is too beautiful to eat.

The parable of the once useful duck whose overweening pride and vanity transformed it into an aesthetic but useless swan has multiple ramifications; it is an emblem of the mother herself in her emigration to the United States in search of a materially more prosperous life, as well as a metaphor of every mother's unrealistic ambitions for her daughter (who is merely a duck but whom the mother wants to see as a swan). Suyuan Woo, for example, possessing enormous faith that everything is possible in America and expecting her child to be a prodigy, first wanted Jing-mei to be another Shirley Temple, and when that seemed unlikely, then at least a concert pianist. Simultaneously touching and ludicrous, such dreams characterize the bittersweet tone of the mother-daughter relationships in this book, as they did in ⟨Maxine Hong Kingston's⟩ *The Woman Warrior*. The daughters are proud of their mothers' strength and ingenuity; moved by their tragic, beautiful stories from the Old Country, and touched by their fierce love; but at the same time the daughters are exasperated by their mothers' impossible demands; resentful of their mothers' intrusions on their lives, and sometimes humiliated and ashamed of their stubborn, superstitious, out-of-place Old World ways.

—Amy Ling, *Between Worlds: Women Writers of Chinese Ancestry* (New York: Pergamon Press, 1990), 131–33

ANGELS CARABI

Caribi: Do you see any common threads with other women belonging to ethnic groups?

Tan: I think there is more of a history of suffering, of pain, of hardships among ethnic women writers. Writers of different ethnic backgrounds or writers who have very different voices—southern writers, even, in the United States—have had very painful, tragic experiences in their lives. If our parents came from another country, we may feel at some point that we can never become as Chinese, as Mexican, or whatever, as our parents. We feel shame about not even wanting to attempt to know the culture, because we've fallen so far behind. I felt that for a while. I would never attempt to speak Chinese to people because I thought, "Oh, they're going to say, 'Her Chinese is so bad. How could she ever be Chinese?' " I have friends that feel the same way. Now I try; I'm more open to possibilities now. You have to lose that shame, which is really a perception of your own limitation. When you're from a different ethnic group, you may perceive that you can only fulfill your potential in one particular culture and not both. And you end up choosing. Some people might say, "If you really are serious about literature, you have to prove that you're a writer by not writing about Chinese-American things." As if you have to choose one or the other. You have to choose what feels right within you. My writing is both American literature and about Chinese aspects of life. ⟨. . .⟩

Caribi: Do your stories have a mythical quality?

Tan: The old tales have a magic of their own. Within personal stories, you can have a mythical quality also with magical, unexpressed meanings. People have told me that my book has myth-like elements. I suppose it's that fairy tale convention of somebody needing to tell a story for a reason. I like the idea of a story for which it's not always clear what you learned at the end, at least not intellectually. One story in *The Joy Luck Club* came about through an image. In "Magpies," the mother recounts a story about magpies who eat tears. There is no real story like that, although these birds are called "birds of happiness." There's something strange about seeing a lot of birds together loudly proclaiming and clacking their mouths. I just said, "OK, let's make up a story about this." It just created itself by my looking at images. But I don't think there are any myths about those birds. Sometimes I've been told related things by people. They'll say, "Did you know that in China this signified that and you were able to capture this?" I think that's because certain symbols in our lives are universal or instinctual within all of us.

—Angels Carabi, "Belles Lettres Interview: Amy Tan," *Belles Lettres* 7, no. 1 (Fall 1991): 18–19

MALINI JOHAR SCHUELLER

Tan's construction of ethnic identity is not based on a vision of a stable and unchanging China that can be recalled at will. Although the theme of estrangement from, and unification with, cultural origins is integral to the work, these origins are multiple and discursive. Part of Tan's purpose in having four different Chinese-born mothers is to introduce different versions of China, neither of which is prioritized over the other. At the most obvious level, there are clear class differences among the mothers' experiences of China. Auntie Lin's family in China revels in consumerism, surrounding itself with color TV sets and remote controls; An-Mei Hsu's family, on the other hand, is awed at having a relative in the land of consumer goods. More importantly, for the American-born daughters, the Chinese past exists discursively, in language, through the stories told about it by their mothers. Ethnic origins, in other words, are always already complicated by representation. 〈. . .〉 The most interesting example of ethnic origins being based on multiple and changing representations is the history of the Joy Luck Club itself. Suyan Woo tells her daughter the history of the Joy Luck Club which she started in Kweilin, but the history changes with each retelling. Her daughter, who has heard the story many times, never thinks her mother's Kweilin story about the origins of the Joy Luck Club is "anything but a Chinese fairy tale. The endings always changed. Sometimes she said she used that worthless thousand-yuan note to buy a half-cup of rice. She turned that rice into a pot of porridge. . . . The story always grew and grew" (25). In many ways, the club itself deconstructs traditionally perceived oppositions between history and fiction, the experiential and the discursive. The club is formed as a make-believe celebration of plenty during the devastation of Japanese occupation and thus has a fictive function. Yet the club survives as Suyan Woo's most "real" memory of the war period. The club is based on stories, "stories spilling out all over the place" (24). The women tell each other stories about "good times in the past and good times yet to come," pretending each week is a new year, and this self-consciously fictive club becomes the basis for creating an immigrant community in California.

Similarly, Tan's mode of narration questions the very idea of historical context as something that can be retrieved through a recording of facts. Tan uses a dialogic mixture of myth, fantasy, reverie, and historical facts without demarcating any as more true than the other and thus questions the truth status of a national history. Within "true" stories of the Chinese past of immigrant mothers, stories of arranged marriages and Japanese occupation, there are affective images of mythical women like the Moon Lady and grotesque images of destructive mothers dismembering their daughters. The concept of a Chinese woman's identity, Tan suggests, is a discursive one. Similarly, the last section of the book, which includes four narratives of mothers and daughters coming to an understanding, is titled "Queen Mother of the Western Skies" and obviously invokes the figure of Queen Mother, the feminization of Buddha who appears (in White Lotus Buddhism) as the creator of mankind and the controller of time. The blend of myth and traditional historical story-telling that informs the narratives about China suggests that ethnic origins are always created and recreated in the complex process of social representation. To think of ethnicity as an essence is to fall prey to the fortune cookie syndrome, to create monologic definitions in order to manage differences. As An-Mei Hsu tells Lindo Jong about fortune cookies, "American people think Chinese people write these sayings." "But we never say such things!" I said. "These things don't make sense" (262).

Tan's simultaneous use of the motif of the return to origins and her complication of these origins raises a matter of unquestionable importance for women of color. Is it desirable for a radical feminist politics to view femininity and ethnicity as ever-changing social constructs? Is it possible to demand and affect social change without the construction of a whole and unified subject? The answer to both those questions has to be a yes if only because the alternatives are so dangerous. As an example of the problems inherent in momentarily positing a singular ethnicity and femininity we can look, for a moment, at Tan's text. The last chapter of *The Joy Luck Club* presents an idealized moment of ethnic identity, set deliberately against the multiplicities of the rest of the novel. The chapter concerns Jing-Mei Woo's trip to China to meet her two half-sisters whom her mother was forced to abandon and who have been miraculously located by the members of the Joy Luck Club. The trope of the lost motherland and the lost mother become one here. Jing-Mei Woo feels herself "becoming" Chinese as the train crosses the border from Hong Kong. "Once you are born Chinese, you cannot help but feel and think Chinese. . . . It is in your blood" (267). The entire chapter enacts a rhapsody of ethnic identity as Jing-Mei and her father meet old relatives and finally the two lost sisters. Here Jing-Mei Woo understands an ethnic identity that is beyond language: "And now I also see what part of me is Chinese. It is so obvious. It is my family. It is in our blood. After all these years, it can finally be let go" (288). But while Tan celebrates this moment of ethnic wholeness, she is also aware of the problems that such essentialist concepts pose. Moments such as these deny the class differences between the tourist gazer and the ethnic subject and suggest an ethnic oneness that the text thus far has questioned. Tan therefore chooses to end her narrative not with this moment but with a commentary on it. The text ends with Jing-Mei and her sisters looking at a Polaroid photo of themselves that Jing-Mei's father has just taken, and with Jing-Mei recognizing her mother in the composite of the three sisters. Jing-Mei recognizes an ethnic identification but only through her active interpretation and by deliberately framing ethnic "subjects" in a momentary stasis beyond language.

—Malini Johar Schueller, "Theorizing Ethnicity and Subjectivity: Maxine Hong Kingston's *Tripmaster Monkey* and Amy Tan's *The Joy Luck Club*," *Genders* 15 (Winter 1992): 81–82

MARINA HEUNG

In ⟨*The Joy Luck Club*⟩ the daughters understand Chinese, but they speak English exclusively. The mothers, in contrast, speak ⟨. . .⟩ a *patois* of Chinese and English that often confuses their daughters. Observing her aunties, June thinks: "The Joy Luck aunties begin to make small talk, not really listening to each other. They speak in their special language, half in broken English, half in their own Chinese dialect" (p. 34). Embarrassing at times to the daughters, this language is a form of self-inscription in an alien culture, a way of preserving significance in the new reality of America. For one, the nuggets of foreign words incorporated into this speech duplicate aspects of self-identity that have no equivalent in another language. Words like *libai, chuming*, and *nengkan* must remain in their original Chinese in order to retain their power and meaning. For Ying-Ying, the essence of her youthful character before she became a lost soul, a "ghost," is contained in the word *libai*: "When I was a young girl in Wushi, I was *libai*. Wild and stubborn. I wore a smirk on my face. Too good to listen" (p. 243). Her confidence in her special knowledge is expressed by *chuming*, referring to her "inside knowledge of things" (p. 248). For Rose, *nengkan* expresses her mother's ability to act on pure will and determination, as shown in An-Mei's summoning of her son's spirit after he has drowned at the beach (pp. 121–31). On another occasion, An-Mei's command of this hybrid language enables her to articulate, on her daughter's behalf, Rose's disorientation during her divorce. When An-Mei complains that Rose's psychiatrist is making her *hulihudu* and *heimongmong*, Rose ponders: "It was true. And everything around me seemed to be *heimongmong*. These were words I have never thought about in English terms. I suppose the closest in meaning would be 'confused' and 'dark fog' " (p. 188).

⟨. . .⟩ Without being overtly political or subversive, the mothers' bilingualism in the novel is nonetheless strategic. Switching from English to Chinese can express rejection and anger, as when June's mother berates her for not trying hard enough at her piano playing: " 'So ungrateful,' I heard her mutter in Chinese. 'If she had as much talent as she has temper, she would be famous now' " (p. 136). Or, the switching of codes may initiate a shift into a different register of intimacy, as when the same mother speaks in Chinese when making her daughter a gift of a jade pendant (p. 208). To express her resentment against an American husband who persistently puts English words in her mouth, Ying-Ying uses Chinese exclusively with her daughter (p. 106). Deliberate deformations of language, too, are used to convey veiled criticisms, as when Ying-Ying snidely refers to her daughter's profession as an architect as "arty-tecky" (p. 242), and An-Mei dismisses Rose's psychiatrist as "psyche-tricks" (p. 188). Finally, the use of Chinese is a form of resistance to a hegemonic culture. ⟨. . .⟩

In *The Joy Luck Club*, "multilanguedness" bears the imprint of their speakers' unique cultural positioning, but this assertion of difference is also vexed by its potential to confuse and exclude. For the daughters, the special meaning of maternal language requires translation. After her mother's death, June thinks: "My mother and I never really understood each other. We translated each other's meanings and I seemed to hear less than what was said, while my mother heard more" (p. 37). Another question is how effectively maternal language functions as a medium of transmission between generations. The mothers in the novel worry that the family history and knowledge preserved in their hybrid language will be elided after their deaths. At one point, June comes to understand how important it is for her aunties to preserve the meaning of "joy luck": "They see that joy and luck do not mean the same to their daughters, that to these closed American-born minds 'joy luck' is not a word, it does not exist. They see daughters who will bear grandchildren born without any connecting hope from generation to generation" (pp. 40–41).

Hybrid in its origins, maternal language in *The Joy Luck Club* possesses multiple, even contradictory, meanings. As an assertion of cultural identity, it both communicates and obfuscates. At the same time, it stands in counterpoint to maternal silence. To the daughters, maternal silence hints at "unspeakable tragedies" (p. 20), and the maternal injunction to "bite back your tongue" (p. 89) binds daughters and mothers in a cycle of self-perpetuating denial. Yet both daughters and mothers resist this bind. The Joy Luck aunties, after all, plead frantically with June to tell her mother's—and, by implication, their own—history ("Tell them, tell them"). ⟨. . .⟩

In the tradition of breaking silence that has become one of the shaping myths in the writings of women of color, maternal silence in the novel is transformed from a medium of self-inscription and subjectivity into an instrument of intersubjectivity and dialogue. For the mothers, storytelling heals past experiences of loss and separation; it is also a medium for rewriting stories of oppression and victimization into parables of self-affirmation and individual empowerment. For the Joy Luck mothers, the construction of a self in identification with a maternal figure thus parallels, finally, a revisioning of the self through a reinterpretation of the past.

    —Marina Heung, "Daughter-Text/Mother-Text: Matrilineage in Amy Tan's *Joy Luck Club*," *Feminist Studies* 19, no. 3 (Fall 1993): 604–7

LESLIE BOW

The Joy Luck Club is an aesthetically pleasing novel; its resolution satisfyingly complete. Its convincing and humorous portrayal of the relationship between mothers and daughters is an important part of its emotional resonance. Tan's novel highlights the complex, often ambivalent relationship between mothers and daughters and an important source of women's community. An accessible work, it is easy to "relate to" given the apparent universality of the mother/daughter experience. Additionally, the positive effect of having Amy Tan's voice out in a mainstream literary market, which is only just beginning to see Asian American literature as more than *The Woman Warrior*, cannot be denied.

    However, the content and circumstances surrounding *The Joy Luck Club* can suggest larger issues about ideological interpretation and the dissemination of Asian American literary texts. *The Joy Luck Club* seems eminently marketable because it presents American ethnic angst as privatized and familial, and thereby addresses issues of race in a non-threatening manner. This is not to critique the text for what it is not, but it is fair to pose the question, "How will Tan's success affect subsequent Asian American writers who might hold more overtly political or culturally nationalist views?" In being seen as less commodifiable, will they get "Amy Tan" rejection slips like those that exhort budding writers to "write more like Kingston"? Also, because Tan's book lends itself to feminist interpretation, will it be subject to white feminist coopting, readings that continually foreground questions of gender over those of racial identity? ⟨. . .⟩

    In a 1989 article, journalist Edward Iwata suggests that the recent commodification of Asian American literature may influence Asian American writers to deflate overt political content in order to court a mainstream audience. In reference to the rising commercial stars of Asian American literature, Amy Tan among them, perennial critic Frank Chin comments, "They're bright and literate, but they still don't confront the issues of what it means to be an Asian

American . . . They're still ornamental Orientals, the latest talking chimps that can talk sign language" (in Edward Iwata, "Hot Properties," 1989).

Talking chimps aside, can it be said that this literary pandering is necessary for marketability? In discussing the narratival displacement of conflict in Tan's novel, I do not intend to suggest that dissent is entirely contained. Negotiating the complex relationship between race and gender through narrative is precisely to confront "issues of what it means to be an Asian American." By making this argument, I hope to avoid the dichotomy that Shirley Lim suggests is posited by the editors of *Aiiieeeee!*, Frank Chin, Jeffrey Paul Chan, Lawson Fusao Inada, and Shawn Hsu Wong, in their insistence on "real" and "fake" ethnicity. Lim writes, "To delegitimate the literary criteria that privileged white mainstream writing and marginalized ethnic literature, the *Aiiieeeee!* critics set up an alternate critical hegemony for Asian American writing based on masculinist and sociological evaluation" ("Japanese American Women's Life Stories: Maternality in Monica Sone's *Nisei Daughter* and Joy Kogawa's *Obasan*," 1990, 290). Here, I hope to avoid setting up criteria for Asian American literary authenticity based on degrees of resistant consciousness. Cultural critic Stuart Hall writes that "we formulate our intentions within ideology" but that the media, and by extension, literary texts, are yet not "simply the ventriloquists of a unified and racist 'ruling class' conception of the world" ("The Whites of Their Eyes: Racist Ideologies and the Media," 1981, 35). Given this tension, all texts must be understood as being simultaneously contained within ideological constructions of race and gender even at the moment that the deformation of those categories can be read into them. What is interesting about *The Joy Luck Club* is that the very process of its envisioning an oppositional mode of being based on feminine connection seems to deflate its cultural specificity.

By containing a racial discourse within a feminist one, Tan's novel allows her characters to reach identity resolution without confronting their racial difference. Instead, the novel mystifies racial subject formation by portraying it as a matter of blood ties and displacing it onto what Alice Walker praises on the book jacket as "the mystery of the mother-daughter bond." Given the ease of her introduction into the literary marketplace—perhaps attributable to a narrative "sneak attack" in containing questions of ethnic difference within a "universal" feminist resolution—Amy Tan may have been following the advice of one of her characters: "Wise guy, he not go against wind . . . Strongest wind cannot be seen" (89).

—Leslie Bow, "Cultural Conflict/Feminist Resolution in Amy Tan's *The Joy Luck Club*," *New Visions in Asian American Studies: Diversity, Community, Power*, ed. Franklin Ng et al. (Pullman, WA: Washington State University, 1994), 245–46

CLAIRE MESSUD

The tremendous success of Amy Tan's two previous novels, "The Joy Luck Club" and "The Kitchen God's Wife," lay in her capacity to evoke, vividly and with subtle humor, the cultural dislocation of America's Chinese community. She has conjured the tortuous lives of an older generation of women whose fate brought them from China to this country, as well as the frustration and fascination of their American-born daughters. It is not surprising, then, that in her latest book, "The Hundred Secret Senses," she should offer an apparent reworking of this theme.

However, rather than focusing again on the mother-daughter bond, Ms. Tan has shifted her attention slightly, choosing this time an exploration of sisterhood. Olivia Bishop, a commercial photographer, is the novel's primary narrator. She is the child of an irresponsible American mother and a Chinese father who died when Olivia was almost 4. Kwan, her half sister, is 12 years her senior, the product of their father's first marriage in China; she appeared in Olivia's life when Olivia was still a small child. Theirs is not, from the younger sister's perspective, an easy relationship: Kwan is eccentric, naïve and annoying. She "believes she has yin eyes," Olivia tells us. "She sees those who have died and now dwell in the World of Yin." She also holds conversations with these ghosts, a habit that landed her in a mental institution not long after her arrival in America. 〈. . .〉

〈. . .〉 She is intent on reuniting Olivia with her estranged husband, Simon, and luring the pair to China, to her native village of Changmian. But her most ambitious goal is a spiritual one: to encourage her sister to acknowledge the reality of the World of Yin and the truth of reincarnation. 〈. . .〉

〈. . .〉 At the novel's conclusion, Olivia gushes: "The world is not a place but the vastness of the soul. And the soul is nothing more than love, limitless, endless, all that moves us toward knowing what is true. . . . And believing in ghosts—that's believing that love never dies."

The dislocation Ms. Tan exposes here is not so much between the Chinese and the American experience—although Olivia initially assumes it to be so—as between a mystical and a pragmatic world view. (Upon her arrival in China, Olivia discovers that while Kwan's friends there may be more tolerant of her communion with the spirits, they don't necessarily believe in it.) In appealing to Olivia's—and the reader's—uinacknowledged mystical urges, Ms. Tan taps a rich but risky source: our relationship to the dead is also a measure of our connection to life itself, and Kwan's belief in eternal cosmic renewal is enticing.

The difficulty arises from Ms. Tan's determination to make actual the links between past and present lives. In the face of physical evidence, Olivia comes to believe not only in the spiritual truth of Kwan's visions but in their literal truth: hence her cringe-making exclamations about love, the soul and ghosts.

To accept the novel as anything more than a mildly entertaining and slightly ridiculous ghost story, the reader must also make this demanding leap of faith, turning a blind eye to rash improbabilities and a host of loose ends. For this reader, at least, that leap was not possible. Even Olivia's conversion fails to convince.

Nonetheless, Kwan, in particular, is a memorable creation. Of *her* belief in the World of Yin there can be no doubt. She emerges as a character at once innocent and wise, the relative Olivia both suffers and relies upon. Kwan gently forces Olivia to face the worst in herself and, in so doing, to find her strengths. We could all do with such a sister.

—Claire Messud, "Ghost Story," *The New York Times Book Review* (29 October 1995): 11

WENDY HO

Another way of accessing ⟨*The Joy Luck Club*⟩ is to analyze ⟨Tan's⟩ use of traditional Chinese legends (for example, the Moon Lady story) and images to articulate the concerns of Chinese American women. For instance, the Joy Luck mothers want their daughters to turn into beautiful swans—perfect, happy, successful, and independent women. In traditional Chinese stories, swans symbolize married, heterosexual love. Tan subverts and re-interprets the traditional image of swans by applying it to the silenced and intimate pairings between women. In this case, a mother and her daughter. The traditional symbols and narratives are being appropriated, reconstructed, or ruptured by writers like Tan (and Maxine Hong Kingston) who do not wish to focus on the master narratives of patriarchy, but to focus instead on the powerful stories of love and struggle between mothers and daughters, between women in China and in America. The stories in *The Joy Luck Club* give voice to the desires and experiences of female characters who have not had the advantage to write or tell their stories as men have had. It is their neglected stories that they tell and attempt to transmit to their daughters in the oral traditions of talk-story. These hybrid talk-story narratives challenge those who would deny or lessen the power, beauty, value, and pain in these women's lives. This is what Maxine Hong Kingston spent a lot of time learning in her memoir *The Woman Warrior*: "The reporting is the vengeance—not the beheading, not the gutting, but the words" (63). The personal stories of the Joy Luck mothers do battle through gossip, circular talking, cryptic messages/caveats, dream images, bilingual language, and talk-story transitions—not in the linear, logical, or publicly authorized discourse in patriarchal or imperialist narratives. This is talk that challenges the denial of Asian American women's voices and identities—denials not only by a male-dominated Chinese society and a Eurocentric American society but also by their very own daughters who have become so

Americanized that they can barely talk-story with their mothers. In many ways, Tan's book can be fruitfully compared with *The Woman Warrior*. As heroic paper daughters in quest of their mothers' stories, Tan and Kingston empower not only their mothers but also themselves and their racial/ethnic communities through a psychic and oral/literary birthing that keeps alive the intimate, ever-changing record of tragedies, resistances, and joy luck for all people.

   —Wendy Ho, "Swan-Feather Mothers and Coca-Cola Daughters: Teaching Amy Tan's *The Joy Luck Club*," *Teaching American Ethnic Literatures: Nineteen Essays*, ed. John R. Maitino and David R. Peck (Albuquerque: University of New Mexico, 1996), 338–39

DIANE FORTUNA

In ⟨. . .⟩ *The Hundred Secret Senses*, Tan tries her hand at magic realism—a contemporary term that derives from Hawthorne's definition of the romance: a tale that takes place where the actual and the imaginary meet. This reincarnation moves back and forth between the commercialized and bland American present, to the fascinating and brutal time of the T'ai P'ing rebellion in the 1850's. (San Francisco in the 1990's with its Chinese take-out food, bargain shopping and marital separations pales before descriptions of Southern China and the emergence of the Heavenly King, who, with his God worshippers and foreign mercenaries, warred for more than a decade against the entire Manchu Dynasty.) ⟨. . .⟩

Readers of historical romances, those who use the psychic network, students of parapsychology, believers in extraterrestrial life forms and fans of "X-Files" will like this book. What most commends the novel are the fragments of actual Chinese history, so exotically retrieved that the reader hurries through the modern narrative in order to learn more about the past. Tan, moreover, has an impeccable ear for both contemporary West Coast speech and Chinese-American dialect. When she juxtaposes the two, the results are often comic. Her canvas, however, seems limited to the relationships between Chinese and Chinese-American mothers and daughters. In *The Hundred Secret Senses*, Olivia consciously refers to Kwan as a surrogate mother. The men, in contrast, are either unaccountably mysterious or downright villainous or just unrealized: Olivia's father has abandoned his Chinese wife and child, and like Nemo, has no name; Captain Crane betrays the Heavenly King and the Changmian Christians without explanation, and Simon does not develop, in either of his manifestations, beyond a plastic foil for the women who know and tell all.

   —Diane Fortuna, [Review of *The Hundred Secret Senses*], *America* 174, no. 15 (4 May 1996): 27–28

BIBLIOGRAPHY

The Joy Luck Club. 1989.
The Kitchen God's Wife. 1991.
The Moon Lady. 1992.
The Chinese Siamese Cat. 1994.
The Hundred Secret Senses. 1995.

Linda Ty-Casper

b. 1931

LINDA TY-CASPER was born on September 17, 1931, in Manila, the Philippines. Her father, a civil engineer, and mother, an educator and writer, hoped that their daughter would become a doctor or a lawyer. Though the future novelist did graduate from law school, she records feeling the desire to write as early as the age of five.

After graduating from the University of the Philippines, where she earned a degree in law, Linda married Leonard R. Casper, a professor and writer, with whom she subsequently had two daughters. In 1956, the couple moved to Boston, where Ty-Casper enrolled in Harvard Law School and began writing short stories. While awaiting bar exam results, she began systematically to read the books about the Philippines in the Harvard library. Finding them full of misinformation and colonialist perspectives, she was inspired to redress this view of her homeland in a revisionist historical novel, *The Peninsulars*. Unfortunately, it remained unpublished until after the release of her first collection of short stories, *The Transparent Sun and Other Stories*, in 1963.

Subsequent novels, short stories, and articles have drawn critical praise for their lyricism despite Ty-Casper's delving into the disturbing and often brutal realities of Filipino society, from a 300-year history of colonization and political corruption to the trauma of exile and repatriation. Real incidents, like the bombing of Plaza Miranda in Manila and the overthrow of the Marcos regime, frequently provide the material or structure of her stories. Writing about the people and places of her native country, Ty-Casper also interweaves basic elements of life and humanity—love, death, family, survival, freedom.

Ty-Casper periodically teaches writing workshops and publishes in magazines and newspapers in the United States and abroad. She was a Fellow at Silliman University in 1963 and at the Radcliffe Institute in 1974 to 1975, and a writer in residence at the University of the Philippines in 1980 and 1982. Her work has appeared in many anthologies, including *Best American Short Stories of 1977*. In 1985, she received a literature award from the Filipino American Women's Network, and in 1986, *Awaiting Trespass* was selected for inclusion in the Feminist Book Fortnight of Britain and Ireland.

CRITICAL EXTRACTS

NINOTCHKA ROSCA

Since the arrival of the Spaniards in 1521, Filipinos have frequently lived in years of the Chinese curse—that is, during "important times." The wise Chinese viewed eras of decisive national development as "cursed," in that they do not permit the individual to maintain a normal lifestyle. At such times one is swept along into vast movements over which, quite often, one has no control; one's life is taken out of one's hands and given over to the tortuous workings of history.

Linda Ty-Casper's novel ⟨The Three-Cornered Sun⟩ deals with one such year, perhaps the most important yet in Philippine history—1896, when the germinal national consciousness became an active force and exploded into Asia's first anti-colonial war of liberation. The subject is not unique to Ty-Casper's book. Most Filipino writers have found the theme inescapable; it constitutes the single, overwhelming "nightmare"—as Marx called the past—that weighs on the minds of living Filipinos.

The Ty-Casper novel, then, is a welcome addition to the growing lore concerning those times, which affected and continue to mold the contemporary Filipino world view. However, her novel is different from many others of this genre in that it attempts to recreate those times, dramatizing the tensions of the 1896 revolution against Spain and delineating its subjective meaning to individuals as opposed to its objective meaning in history.

Because the Ty-Casper characters live within those "important times," the link between their essentially Filipino consciousness and Spain is strong and fresh. We are therefore able to witness the severing of this link and the growth of another weltanschauung in its place. It is not an easy process, because Spain and its traditions, habits of thought, and manners had dominated the archipelago for nearly 300 years. The mental torments of those involved in the revolution (was it sanctioned by God, or was God a Spaniard?) take precedence over the physical torments of the war itself. Indeed, this makes for overly self-conscious characters who subject each of their actions and decisions to internal debate.

But that is the novel's purpose: not to chart the revolution as a battle map but as a slow thrust toward the light of a new consciousness—one that can call itself Filipino, resolving in the acceptance of that name its dilemmas vis-à-vis Spain and the God who came in the guise of a Spaniard. The formulation of a new ideology is as important as the actual winning of the war itself.

Because this is the novel's central theme, it is inevitable that the characters are peripheral to the decision-making bodies of the revolution. This way, they do not become directly involved in the political problems of the war; rather, they interpret and reinterpret the revolution in terms of their own individual perspectives. It is to Ty-Casper's credit that the novel makes use of the archetypal elements of the Filipino character without their falling into clichés. Reasons for joining the revolution run the gamut of the Filipino's strengths and weaknesses: they range from petty ambition to the metaphysical attempt to define one's character. We encounter persons who are familiar to us because they represent a particular "bent" of the Filipino and have appeared many times in Philippine literature: the self-indulgent man, the society queen bee, the rich who delude themselves as to their importance, the déclassé intellectual who lives with the poor of the revolution but who remains apart by virtue of his knowledge, the mystic-soldier-priest who is responsible for defining what is moral, and the academician who withdraws from action into the hieroglyphics of philosophy.

It is ironic that in the midst of a mass movement we should find souls who are isolated and unable to establish profound relationships with those around them. Ultimately it is the poor, the untutored, who focus the revolution's ideals into concrete individual sacrifice, for examples, Palma drawing Spanish gunfire away from Cristobal, the old man Ipe refusing to betray the revolutionists, and Amado drawing a soldier's anger away from Cristobal. At that level, the nobility of the revolution is made manifest, forming an effective contrast to the obsession with death characteristic of the intellectuals in the novel.

The novel ends at a rare moment, which more than makes up for the difficulties that the prose style presents. Ty-Casper's prose is heavy and slow; the awkwardness of her sentence structures, her use of alliteration, and her overuse of adjectives can be irritating. Sometimes, too, the novelist's eye falters, as where she writes that "he saw the faces of those occupying the *bleaching* boards" (my emphasis), resulting in confused word-images. But this is one book whose content and grandeur of theme render such faults minor. For those interested in the Philippines or even in gaining a limited understanding of the Third World viewpoint, *The Three-Cornered Sun* is a good beginning.

—Ninotchka Rosca, [Review of *The Three-Cornered Sun*], *The Journal of Asian Studies* 40, no. 4 (August 1981): 859–60

CELIA GILBERT

Despite the historical matrix out of which Ty-Casper's work comes it would be a mistake to think of her as only a historical, or political, novelist. Ty-Casper characterizes herself as an independent, perhaps one perpetually in opposition. Her commitment is to exploring the ways in which men and women must struggle to resist the erosions of worldly corruption, to preserve their integrity. Like all of her work, *Awaiting Trespass* asks us to look at a moment when the individual makes choices which involve life or death for the self—or to put it in old-fashioned terms, the soul.

If in particular we want to know how nuns came to sit down before tanks, how unarmed civilians put flowers in loaded gun barrels, how the Comelec women armed only with their conscience defied the government rather than be party to election fraud, or why thousands of people rallied to the yellow colors of the so-called "housewife" Cory Aquino, we can do no better than to study this paradigmatic story of an upper-class Filipino clan confronting the realities of their moment in history. At the same time it is because Ty-Casper knows so well how to create living characters that we are held and moved by the transformation of her two finely imagined protagonists, Sevi, the priest son of Don Severino, unsure of his vocation, and Telly, the Don's lonely and rebellious niece, a would-be poet, as both of them search for a way to live lives of love and connectedness.

The ever-widening reflections the book provokes take the reader into a meditation on the destiny of small countries doomed by history to repeated intervention at the hands of larger ones. It throws into relief for American readers our own part in events, little taught and rarely recalled, that have formed the experience of so much of the world. ⟨. . .⟩

Although I believe Ty-Casper is by temperament spiritually a protestant writer, that is not to deny her deep Catholic roots. It is, however, a Catholicism that is very Filipino in origin. From the beginning, when the Spanish Church distributed Bibles to the laity as a way of teaching the people not to rebel, the Filipinos seized on the emblem of Christ's passion to stand for their own national humiliation and pain: this at a time when no Filipino was allowed to be a priest. Later, a national Catholic church was formed for that very reason. As one of the characters in the book declares, "Saving ourselves is possible because Christ came into history. If we believe in Him, we will not tolerate absolute rulers on earth. We will resist . . ." There is no doubt that this widely shared feeling underlay the unanimity of the bishops in standing up finally to the Vatican as well as to Marcos and throwing their full weight to the opposition.

Much of the impulse behind Ty-Casper's desire to write came from her maternal grandmother and her stories of the rebellion against Spain in 1896. It was to her she dedicated *The Three-Cornered Sun*, a full-length novel written in 1979, more relevant than ever today. Here she chronicles her characters, once again members of a family that mirrors the internecine strife of the country, caught in the toils of doubt and daily perils, in small skirmishes, small betrayals, shifting allegiances and dire uncertainties about the outcome of their hopes. Although her stance is resolutely antiheroic, Ty-Casper speaks, too, for those who find in the revolutionary situation an enchantment they long for, "a force [that] drives people through their lives, connecting them, transforming them to their utmost. Through it they had tasted eternity." It is a tribute to the power of Ty-Casper's own quiet but deeply felt ideas of justice and morality that these words ring so movingly at the end of the book.

—Celia Gilbert, "Transforming Fact into Fiction," *The Women's Review of Books* 3, no. 10 (July 1986): 8

SUZANNE SCOTT AND LYNNE M. CONSTANTINE

⟨Scott/Constantine:⟩ Your style is so clear and musical. Do you write poetry? ⟨. . .⟩

⟨Ty-Caspar:⟩ ⟨. . .⟩ I use a lot of simple, clear imagery in my work. Philippine writing in general has a lot of metaphors. The national language is very metaphoric because we have had to mask what we felt, both for political reasons and so as not to offend. When I use an image, it's usually one that I've taken from life. For example, the scene of the bird caught in the web which I used in *Wings of Stone* actually happened. There was a very big mango tree outside, and I thought I saw a leaf moving in a strange way. When I asked my cousin George to look at that leaf, he discovered it was a little sparrow caught in a big spider web. When I write, I remember things like that. ⟨. . .⟩

⟨Scott/Constantine:⟩ Do you think your fiction has an impact on how people look at events in your country?

⟨Ty-Caspar:⟩ Books do tend to change people, and fiction, I think, changes people more than nonfiction does. I think that's why many people find it dangerous. You can read the newspaper and forget about it. But when you read fiction, it stays with you. When a friend of mine read *Awaiting Trespass*, she said to me, "That's a tough book." And I hated to tell her that I had written another book that was even tougher. I wanted to protect her.

⟨Scott/Constantine:⟩ Do you find them tough to write, too?

⟨Ty-Caspar:⟩ Oh yes. That's why I think I'll write one more book about the present and then, forget it, that's it. I'll go back to 1899. I think I should write about the revolution of 1899; to the Filipino people, it's something like the curse of Vietnam. Filipinos have done very little writing about the 1899 revolution. In 1974, I wrote two short stories about it and sent them out to magazines. I got lots of rejections. Sometimes the editors would say, "The soldiers in the story think, and soldiers just don't think." Other times, the editors would say, "Not bad for a woman writing war stories." But they rejected it anyway. If someone else would write about it I'd be happy not to. But no one else is.

—Suzanne Scott and Lynne M. Constantine, "Belles Lettres Interview: Linda Ty-Casper," *Belles Lettres* 2, no. 5 (May/June 1987): 5, 15

LINDA TY-CASPER

⟨Linda Ty-Casper told *Contemporary Authors* the following:⟩ I write on impulse. The first lines of stories come to me in the midst of other things. I work steadily in one sitting until the story needs only to be revised. I do not work every day, for that would make writing a drudgery for me. With novels and novellas, I write one scene at a time, much like short stories.

Events shape each chapter of my novels. I know the event and its public outcome, but I don't know what my characters will do as they re-enact it. I research exhaustively, until I can see the place and feel the time: newspapers, songs, letters to editors, all manner of accounts, including telephone directories, are among my sources. I read novels from the period to get the rhythm of words and sentences as distinguished from the rhythm of life which the details of daily living recreate. Inspired by contemporary crises, my novellas are more like extended short stories.

As I write, I have to make discoveries to be surprised. In a sense, each book is a first book. I try to write each one differently, as if it were being written during the period when the events took place. I try to present a portrait of the country, hence the variety of characters and points of view; and the minimal reference to 'historical' figures who are already much written about.

Although I do not write regularly, I am always ready to write when the temptation comes. In between I deliberately occupy myself with what can be readily put aside, with what does not linger in the mind or compete for attention. I write in English, rather than Pilipino, because that was the language of instruction when I was growing up. It is a matter of being able to write down my thoughts quickly before they flee. But I hope to write more seriously in Pilipino, or, failing in that, to translate my writings. I find English precise and objective, while Pilipino allows me to locate feelings better. Cultural affinities and common language allow a writer to implicate his country more deeply in his work, but our lives are not so small and restricted that they should be expressed only in one language. Instead of dividing us, the languages we use will define our variousness and complexity.

I believe writing provides alternatives, by adding still other 'selves' to literature, that house of our many selves. Because a writer writes, history cannot be entirely rewritten according to the specifications of politicians.

—Deborah A. Straub, ed., *Contemporary Authors* (Detroit: Gale Research, Inc., 1988), 449

MAUREEN HOWARD

Awaiting Trespass: A Passion is a short novel set in the Philippines in 1981. While its form, a canticle of sorrows, draws the story of one death, one family together in a sober eulogy, Linda Ty-Casper's style is mostly brilliantly satiric. Ty-Casper has written several novels, but, so far as I can see, she's never been taken note of in America. It can't be that difficult for a publisher to discover one of our own talented "colonial" writers (her work also comes to us by way of Readers International). What's more, they might have cashed in, for *Awaiting Trespass* is, in part, a close look at privileged life in Manila during the Marcos regime.

Ty-Casper is not concerned with scandal-sheet items and Swiss bank accounts but with the real and terrible despair of those who understand the sticky moral climate they live in. Now that the secrets of Imelda's closets have been exposed to all the world and Cory is, with some difficulty, holding her own, *Awaiting Trespass* might be published in the Philippines.

The dead man in the novel, Don Servino Gil, was rich, powerful, corrupt—a caricature of the swaggering playboy. His sisters, three haughty and pious old ladies who aim to keep the past untarnished, still worship their brother (white linen, flower in his buttonhole) as a godlike male whose worst sins are mere peccadillos. A comic chorus in their black finery, they're as competitive as the aunts in *The Mill on the Floss*, checking out their linens and the stores in their pantries. What they represent is fusty, dead, and laughable, but still a weight that pulls down upon the younger members of the family. Don Servino's son is, not surprisingly, a priest, though even that protest has been co-opted by the great man. Big Daddy, yes, but Ty-Casper is not simplistic: the priest has doubts about his vocation; and Don Servino's favorite niece is a sophisticated divorcée drawn to self-destruction, a poet who puts as little faith in her psychiatrist as she does in a fortune-teller.

I was at once reminded of *Leaf Storm*, Gabriel García Márquez's first story— violent death, coffin center stage, the life of the patriarch assembled from each mourner's reverie—but in its fine arguments between poet and priest, its inclusion of a revolutionary nephew who may be "right on" in his heroics but is only one corner of the puzzle, this novel is more like the mature Márquez of *The Autumn of the Patriarch* in scope and moral complexity. But Manila is not Macondo: *Awaiting Trespass* resists nostalgia, and the novel's lyric swirl is not ahistorical; indeed, there is a clear investment here in the immediate risk of rebellion. The cut of society in this requiem is exactly the world that President Aquino comes from, and her allegiance to it may finally be one of her great problems. It is surprising that we have not heard of Ty-Casper: I can only suppose that *Awaiting Trespass* is too subtle a fiction.

　　—Maureen Howard, "Semi-Samizdat and Other Matters," *The Yale Review* 77, no. 2 (March 1988): 247–48

JOSEPH A. GALDON

Ten Thousand Seeds is ⟨Ty-Casper's⟩ best book to date. It chronicles seven months of Philippine history from September 1898 to March 1899 as witnessed by two young Americans, Edward and Calista Rowbotham, who come to Manila on their honeymoon shortly after Dewey's victory in Manila Bay and are participants in the American conquest of Manila. The novel provides a somewhat different point of view of these historical events, for it views them through the eyes and the actions of two American innocents abroad. "We tried to change things," Calista says, "and perhaps have been the ones changed." The novel asks whether these two Americans, and perhaps all Americans, have "risen above the trifles" of the events in Manila of 1898–99.

The structure of Ty-Casper's superb little novel rests upon a scaffold of interlocking symbols. The basic metaphor is that of the epic journey. The physical journey of the newlyweds Edward and Calista is a paradigm for their own individual journey to maturity and the growth of their marriage. "We'll circle the earth again and again," says Calista. "As often as the sun," Edward replies. This personal journey is played out against the background of the Filipino people's journey toward national independence. Their national journey, epic in its proportions, is mirrored by the equally epic American Civil War, which plays such a large role in the families of both Edward and Calista. The sun and the bells of Manila are almost mythic symbols that recur throughout the novel to underline the journey to freedom. This structure of symbols gives the novel a depth and significance that goes beyond the individual lives of Edward and Calista.

Ty-Casper is in love with people. "History to me is people," she once said in a lecture in Manila. "I keep discovering people, and I want to put them all in my novels." Out of the lives of people—American, Spanish, and Filipino— she has written a novel that records the historical struggle of the Philippine people for individual and national freedom as a reflection of the American odyssey of freedom. In *Ten Thousand Seeds* it becomes more than a national struggle. It is a human struggle: "It's like pruning a tree. It grows ever thicker and more stalwart for the cutting."

—Joseph A. Galdon, [Review of *Ten Thousand Seeds*], *World Literature Today* 62, no. 2 (Spring 1988): 337

MARIANNE VILLANUEVA

Ty-Casper's book ⟨*Wings of Stone*⟩ is certainly gloomy, but there is more to the novel than just a collection of outrages. Mysteries abound: what were the real circumstances surrounding Johnny's birth, and was it he or Martin who was born to a poor, nameless woman in his father's clinic? Will Johnny forsake his American wife for the glamorous socialite, Sylvia Mendez, who makes "powerful rhythms and blunt melodies surge through him, forcing him to shiver where he stood"? Like the plot of a convoluted Filipino movie, there is almost too much here for one novel to handle.

But one cannot fault the quality of the writing. Ty-Casper is a wonderful stylist, and her novel is nothing if not engrossing. Her Manila is an old city, rank with decay. Its churches are "so dark, so old," that even the light in them seems to be "falling apart." There is an aura of sadness about the houses dimly lit with low-wattage bulbs that "burned like a candle going out," and the gardens with their old trees, the "spreading acacias," the large "*macopas,* too old to be shaped by the wind or turned by the sun any longer." In Ty-Casper's Manila, plants and people grow rampant, "stirring with the furtiveness of new life swarming." This fecundity sometimes brings alarming visions, as when Johnny looks up at the branches covering the sky and sees what appear to be "pieces of flesh impaled on the branches by birds, entrails and eyes where insects might have laid their eggs," or when, experiencing the incredible congestion of Manila's streets, Johnny thinks of "Goya's monstrous mouths stuffed with human bodies, the faces decaying in full view, corpses standing up to firing squads: everywhere the coarse imprint of death's celebrations."

Ty-Casper strives for some powerful effects, and if at times she seems to be stretching, it is probably because hindsight has given us a different, more optimistic view of the future of the Philippines. Manila today is under a different government, and if Ty-Casper were writing today, knowing now what we know about the bloodless revolution that toppled Ferdinand Marcos from power, she might have written a different book. But *Wings of Stone* is still powerful material. One has the feeling that her description of some of Manila's most disturbing aspects will be around for a good while longer.

—Marianne Villanueva, [Review of *Wings of Stone*], *The Forbidden Stitch: An Asian American Anthology,* ed. Shirley Lim and Mayumi Tsutakawa (Corvallis, OR: Calyx Books, 1989), 249–50

OSCAR V. CAMPOMANES

Nearly all the emergent ⟨Philippine⟩ writers are women, and this amplitude of women's writing is a development observable for other emergent literatures in the United States and the postcolonial world. ⟨. . .⟩ As Filipino historical crises are intensified by the authoritarian rule of Ferdinand Marcos and its aftermath, history and its countermythic writing become their own forms and visions of return, identity building, and self-recovery.

Linda Ty-Casper returned to early colonial Philippine history and showed the way for this group with *The Peninsulars* (1964). The novel has been critiqued for its "ill-advised" revisions of some historical documents but also commended for setting ⟨a precedent.⟩ In fact, Ty-Casper went on to handle Philippine historical subjects more boldly, seeking to make material out of the moral atrophy and political intrigues that mark the period of authoritarian rule by Marcos (see, for example, *Wings of Stone*, 1986; *Fortress in the Plaza*, 1985). One can profit from examining the intertextuality between Ty-Casper's and Ninotchka Rosca's ventures, specifically as borne out by Rosca's historical novel *State of War* (1988). This novel alerts the reader to Rosca's indebtedness to Ty-Casper's pioneering efforts, establishing certain genealogical links between both writers on the narrative level.

In *The Three-Cornered Sun* (1979), Ty-Casper turns to the Philippine Revolution of 1896 against Spain, creating a somewhat indecisive picture of national identity through the members of the Viardo family, whose individual traits are unevenly endowed with allegorical weight. As N.V.M. Gonzalez notes, the call is for "a depiction of private lives that would encompass Philippine experience within living memory," and as Rosca herself qualifies, "The problem is how to tell a story that was not anybody's story yet was everybody's story" ⟨Gonzalez, "Filipino and the Novel," 962⟩.

—Oscar V. Campomanes, "Filipinos in the United States and Their Literature of Exile," *Reading the Literatures of Asian America*, ed. Shirley Geok-lin Lim and Amy Ling (Philadelphia: Temple University Press, 1992), 70–71

DOLORES DE MANUEL

⟨In some Filipino-American fiction,⟩ arranged marriages ⟨between Filipinos and Americans,⟩ in their confrontation with another set of codes, may be in their own way destructive or productive. The implications are both political and cultural, because these are not the family-arranged and socially sanctioned marriages of traditional practice; instead they are arranged by the individual concerned. They take place to acquire a green card, as a defense against deportation by the U.S government, an attempt to circumvent a rigid legal code and to make the ocean crossing more possible and more permanent. However, to some this use of marriage is a source of guilt over the contravention of a moral code, exposing a form of inner death.

Linda Ty-Casper's novel *Wings of Stone* (1986) shows the conflict in its protagonist, who has married to acquire a green card: "it was fake, his conscience outfaced him: outright fake based on a phony marriage. He, Johnny F. Manalo, had undermined the system by importing corruption. Intending to liberate himself in the United States, he had fouled it instead for himself and for everyone who lived there" (12). Johnny Manalo's overscrupulous sense of guilt comes from the ideals he has learned from his father, a doctor who has dedicated his life to treating the poor. He has no reason to feel culpable towards

Rose Quarter, his wife, whom he treats well and wishes he could love; he calls the marriage "fake" but in many senses it is a real one. Instead, his guilt arises from his having married without love and at remaining in a marriage with a woman who is incapable of sustaining a loving relationship. In this equation of value, the ideal Filipino marriage is seen as one which is based on love and whose purpose is to beget children, not one for a blatant legal purpose. The arranged marriage in Ty-Casper's novel thus becomes a representation of an inner sterility that ensues from the incomplete crossing.

The emptiness of the arranged marriage is personified in the description of Rose Quarter, who leads "a life that seemed full of stillborn hopes" (68). She is psychologically handicapped, on medication "to control her thoughts and emotions" (69). Johnny has thought that he can help her: "For some time he believed that if Rose Quarter had someone she loved, who could make her want to, she would become a butterfly instead of a moth" (69). But he has come to realize that there is no hope for change. He finds this out through his relationships with two Filipino women: Sylvia, whose vitality gives him the impression that "she could just as well have sprouted wings" (64), and his dead mother, whose loving relationship with his father seems to have set his ideals for marriage. The sterility of Johnny's relationship with Rose Quarter shows that he is still bound by the codes of Filipino marriage, that he has not made the crossing; the emptiness of his "fake" marriage is representative of the hollowness of the American experience for him. He has redefined himself in a way that is wrong and repugnant to him. Ty-Casper's analysis of the marriage shows that if the crossing is incomplete and the reconstruction of the self is flawed, then the marriage that takes place within an unstable value system cannot work.

—Dolores de Manuel, "'Across That Ocean Is . . .': Trans-Oceanic Revaluations of Marriage in Filipino American Fiction," *Privileging Positions: The Sites of Asian American Studies*, ed. Gary Y. Okihiro et al. (Pullman, WA: Washington State University Press, 1995), 197–98

B I B L I O G R A P H Y

The Transparent Sun and Other Stories. 1963.
The Peninsulars. 1964.
The Secret Runner and Other Stories. 1974.
The Three-Cornered Sun. 1979.
Dread Empire. 1980.
Hazards of Distance. 1981.

Fortress in the Plaza. 1985.
Awaiting Trespass. 1985.
Wings of Stone. 1986.
Ten Thousand Seeds. 1987.
A Small Garden Party. 1988.

Jade Snow Wong

b. 1919

JADE SNOW WONG was born in 1919 in San Francisco, California, to Hong and Hing Kwai Wong. She grew up in a poor section of the city's renowned Chinatown, bound by the behavior required of women in Chinese culture. Throughout her childhood, she struggled to define herself as an individual against the authority of her parents, her church, and her community. Even though she graduated from high school as class valedictorian, her parents withheld financial support for college because she was female. Nonetheless, a determined Wong attended San Francisco Junior College, supporting herself by working as a cook and housekeeper. She graduated in 1940 with the highest honors.

At 20, Wong enrolled in Mills College on a scholarship and again graduated at the top of her class. From 1943 to 1945, she worked as a secretary with the War Production Board and while there won a National Congressional Award for an essay on the cause of absenteeism. In 1945, she published *Fifth Chinese Daughter*, an autobiographical coming-of-age story recounting her early struggles to reconcile the demands of both Chinese and American cultures. *Fifth Chinese Daughter* became a best-seller and is today considered seminal in the history of Asian-American literature.

An innovative potter and sculptor as well as a writer, Wong has received many awards for her work and opened a ceramic gallery in 1946 in San Francisco's Chinatown. Her pieces are included in collections of both the Metropolitan Museum of Art and the Museum of Modern Art in New York. In 1950, she married Woodrow Ong, with whom she has raised four children and started a travel agency. Wong considers the products of her artistic life a vehicle for creating understanding between Chinese and Americans, yet she is deeply committed to her family and community. In an interview for *Contemporary Authors* she has asserted, "I give priority to women's responsibility for a good home life; hence, I put my husband and four children before my writing or ceramics."

No Chinese Stranger, Wong's second book, published in 1975, details the 30 years of her life after the publication of *Fifth Chinese Daughter*. Largely a collection of travel notes and a summary of events, this book does not offer the same insight into the struggles of second-generation Asian Americans as her first. However, as she describes the paradox of feeling acceptance among the people of China yet rejection as a minority in her native United States, Wong makes a significant statement about identity and assimilation.

Acknowledging her literary contribution, Mills College conferred upon Wong an honorary doctorate of humane letters in 1976. A documentary film was made about her at the same time. Although she has not published other books, Wong is an occasional contributor to such publications as *Holiday* and *Horn Book Magazine* and writes a column in the *San Francisco Examiner*.

CRITICAL EXTRACTS

LOWELL CHUN-HOON

Probably the best-known and most lucidly written autobiography for the study of Chinese-American identity is Jade Snow Wong's classic account of a Chinese girlhood, *Fifth Chinese Daughter*. Published in 1950, it has enjoyed success as a best seller in America as well as being translated into Chinese, Japanese, Thai, German, Austrian, Urdu, Burmese and Indonesian under the auspices of the United States State Department.

Fifth Chinese Daughter is enlightening for a variety of reasons. It is an accurate and vivid account of growing-up in San Francisco Chinatown during the 1920's, 1930's, and 1940's, an entertaining autobiography of a young woman, and the success story of an immigrant member of a minority race in America. Most significant in the present day context, however, is the fact that *Fifth Chinese Daughter* is the story of an education in Chinese values, and the struggle of a Chinese-American to reconcile the conflicts between the values of a minority culture in the larger majority society. Rightly perceived, this unique book is a window not only into the past, but into the present and future as well. To understand it thoroughly is to begin to understand the forces at work shaping the fate of Chinese-American identity.

One of the principal unifying themes of *Fifth Chinese Daughter* is the concept of Chinese cultural authority and the series of confrontations between Jade Snow and her parents over the question of parental authority and filial piety. In American society we have come to accept such confrontations as natural and indeed a necessary part of the maturation process. Children are expected and encouraged to become as independent as possible and are ultimately allowed, at least in theory, to choose their own role in life. In traditional Chinese society this was of course not the case at all, and in Jade Snow Wong's early childhood the traditional Chinese ways are dominant. 〈. . .〉

Jade Snow Wong represents the transition in Chinese-American identity from a purely Chinese emphasis upon rigid obedience to the proscribed Confucian dictates of the situation to a Chinese-American reconcilation which legitimates individual and personal initiative when it is successful in bringing honor to the larger Chinese-American community or a given Chinese-American family. Those values rewarded and deemed successful in American society may replace the pure hierarchies of filial piety and obedience in Confucian thought as the primary criterion for behavior. One might say this is a form of adopting American values of success, in the name of upholding the success of Chinese values.

In evaluating the transitional lifestyle evolved by Jade Snow Wong, we come to what appear to be fundamental contradictions. If the primary means for enhancing, honoring, and promoting Chinese cultural identity remains individual success in a culture which requires individual creativity and initiative then the very values necessary for success and the temporary furtherance of Chinese-American identity simultaneously undermines the traditional Chinese identity rooted in obedience to Confucian authority. To state the problem in its most pessimistic perspective: Chinese identity, when transplanted from China, contains within itself the seeds of its own doom. For instead of succeeding through obeying the dictates of Chinese cultural authority, and restraining his individuality, the Chinese-American succeeds through his own individual initiative.

However, once the notion of individual initiative takes hold, it triggers a potentially irreversible and anarchistic process. If Chinese American identity depends on the reverence of tradition and obedience to the persons and ways of previous Chinese generations, this reverence will inhibit success in America to the extent that it will inhibit creativity and self-assertion. There are people like Jade Snow Wong who can utilize their creativity and independence for the Chinese community and can remain both culturally Chinese and individually successful by American standards.

—Lowell Chun-Hoon, "Jade Snow Wong and the Fate of Chinese-American Identity," *Amerasia Journal* 1, no. 1 (March 1971): 52–53, 61–62

ELAINE H. KIM

Jade Snow Wong is ⟨a⟩ proponent of the notion that Asian Americans are a unique blend of "Asian" and "American" cultures. For Park No-Yong the conciliation was perfectly embodied in the doctrine of the mean, a notion that could be found in both Western (ancient Greek) and Chinese philosophy. For Wong it lies in "personal balance": "Each Chinese American like me has the opportunity to assess his talents, define his individual stature, and choose his personal balance of old and new, Chinese and Western ways, hopefully including the best of both." Paradoxically, a combination of the fundamental aspects of the "best" of both means Western civilization—thought, social relations, creative thinking, mental work, way of life—combined with far less critical and pivotal aspects of Chinese civilization, such as food and holiday celebrations.

Ultimately, through the blending of the "Chinese" and "American" qualities, Wong becomes a mere curiosity to both cultures. She admits that after attending college she feels more like a spectator than a participant in her own community. When she invites her economics class to her father's sewing factory, she feels "suddenly estranged" from "observing the scene with two pair of eyes." When she establishes her pottery business in Chinatown, her wares are purchased and appreciated only by whites; the Chinese buy not one single piece. Both whites and Chinese talk about her while she works as if she were a blind deaf mute, as though she were not even present. In a taped interview twenty-five years after the publication of *Fifth Chinese Daughter*, she admitted that she still felt "unaccepted in Chinatown" because of "lack of understanding" on the part of the Chinese there.

In the end, Wong's response to her particular dilemma as an American-born Chinese was to work harder, to seek comfort in certain aspects of her Chinese identity, and to refuse to admit the existence of discrimination. According to Wong, there is no escape from race prejudice; one must simply decide "how much to accept and utilize." This response marked her as a Chinese American success story.

Wong was encouraged to write *Fifth Chinese Daughter* by English teachers and publishing house editors, who were largely responsible for the final version of the book. The editor who asked her to write the book, Elizabeth Lawrence, cut out two-thirds of the manuscript, and the teacher, Alice Cooper, helped "bind it together again." When asked in an interview whether or not she was satisfied with the final results, Wong replied that she was willing to accept the better judgment of her editors: "Some of the things are missing that I would have wanted in. Then, you know, it's like selling to Gump's or sending to a museum. Everybody has a purpose in mind in what they're carrying out. So, you know, you kind of have to work with them." When asked what had been left out, Wong replied that aspects that were "too personal" had been eliminated by the editors, adding, "I was what, twenty-six then? And you know, it takes maturity to be objective about one's self."

Whether because of the editors or not, the emotional life that Jade Snow Wong might have expressed in her autobiography never fully emerges. We know that she was driven by a "desire for recognition as an individual," a desire she felt was thwarted by her family. We also know that she was almost vengefully anxious to "show everyone" that she could succeed in becoming a model of social propriety. She felt lost in a "sea of neglect and prejudice" at home. But in the end these sporadic glimpses into her emotional life are subordinated to descriptions of Moon Festivals and egg foo yung recipes. The submergence of the self so contradictory to her insistence on individuality is epitomized by her reference to herself in the third person singular throughout the book.

    —Elaine H. Kim, *Asian American Literature: An Introduction to the Writings and Their Social Context* (Philadelphia: Temple University Press, 1982), 70–72

KATHLEEN LOH SWEE YIN AND KRISTOFFER F. PAULSON

⟨. . .⟩ ⟨A⟩ close analysis of *Fifth Chinese Daughter* shows that Wong faces a world as frustrating, fragmented, and confusing as that of ⟨Maxine Hong⟩ Kingston. Furthermore, Wong reveals her successful integration of identities in a masterful blending of the autobiographical and of her natural modesty which is derived from the Chinese culture which demands the literal submergence of the individual. "Even written in English an 'I' book by a Chinese would seem outrageously immodest to anyone raised in the spirit of Chinese propriety" ⟨vii–viii⟩. The result is a rarely used and unusual form—the third person autobiography. So rare is this form that Henry Adams' *The Education of Henry Adams* is the only example that comes readily to mind and appears available for comparison. And like Adams, Wong too treats herself "as the object of a process of education." ⟨. . .⟩

⟨. . .⟩ Throughout *Fifth Chinese Daughter's* third person narrative one is always aware of Wong as simultaneously the protagonist and the author: "But Jade Snow still had to make her own decision" ⟨150⟩. If the sentence were read as it must in an autobiography, "But I still had to make my own decision," the tension of the continuous recognition that both the character and the author are thinking and acting as separate entities and yet are one and the same person completely disappears.

Jade Snow Wong writes the narrative biography of Jade Snow. The singular "I" dissolves and re-emerges transformed and re-created in the objective third-person "she." Jade Snow is once removed from the author, as an objective and fictive character within a novel is once removed from the author, and yet she can not be removed, because the character Jade Snow and the author Jade Snow Wong are one and the same person. Yet the separation has been accomplished. The genius of Wong's form lies in the tension of its inherent paradox. ⟨. . .⟩

⟨. . . Her⟩ bi-cultural narrative will not fit into and cannot be contained within the "strictly autobiographical" form. Her narrative voice breaks the form apart. The division, contradiction, tension, paradox and "bursting" are right there in the form itself. The reader is constantly aware of the divided consciousness of the narrator in the divided voice of author and character. The constant tensions reinforce the dual nature of the narrative voice and constantly make the reader aware of the fragile balance between author and character within one dual but identifiable human being. Jade Snow Wong's choice of form cannot be easily designated because we have no name, no term, to identify the contradictory third person autobiography. And Jade Snow Wong's choice of this very unusual form and divided narrative "voice" arises directly out of her bi-cultural identity. For her to use the "I" form would be to deny the Chinese part of her bi-cultural identity ⟨vii–viii⟩.

What the form compels Wong, or any author, to do is to examine her individual character and her society from without, from an objective and aesthetic distance, as well as from an inner and individual point-of-view. That is, her self-examined individual being is also her objective imaginated fiction. *The Education of Henry Adams* provides comparison. In their third person autobiographies both Adams and Wong treat themselves as fictional characters, submerging the individual ego, the "I," within the influences of the forces which surround them. For Wong the chief forces are the many opposing demands of her Chinese-American heritage.

Fifth Chinese Daughter ⟨. . .⟩ like Adams' *Education*, is a work of the imagination—more a work of creative fiction than a simple transcript of events and facts. Jade Snow is a fully rendered, fictional character whom Wong develops within a structured thematic purpose to depict Jade Snow's successful search for balance within the forces of the fragmented world of Chinese-American women.

Wong chose, as Kingston would thirty years later, an extraordinary literary form, one which effectively renders the divided consciousness of dual-heritage. Wong's achievement, however unheralded and unrecognized, is a foundation stone for ethnic literature, for feminist literature and for American literature.

> —Kathleen Loh Swee Yin and Kristoffer F. Paulson, "The Divided Voice of Chinese-American Narration: Jade Snow Wong's *Fifth Chinese Daughter*," *MELUS* 9, no. 1 (Spring 1982): 53–54, 57–59

AMY LING

Even if one's life is not complicated by parents of different races or by geographic relocations, one cannot escape the between-world condition as a non-white in the United States. Both Jade Snow Wong and Maxine Hong Kingston, a generation later, were born to two Chinese parents in the United States and reared in California Chinatowns, San Francisco and Stockton. And the between-world consciousness is central to their autobiographical texts,

Fifth Chinese Daughter (1945) and *The Woman Warrior* (1976). Though Jade Snow Wong's autobiography has been disparaged by a number of Asian American commentators, Kingston herself considers Jade Snow Wong a literary mentor, describing her as "the Mother of Chinese American literature" and the only Chinese American author she read before writing her own book. "I found Jade Snow Wong's book myself in the library, and was flabbergasted, helped, inspired, affirmed, made possible as a writer—for the first time I saw a person who looked like me as a heroine of a book, as a maker of a book."

The two books are greatly divergent in style and temperament, each text largely affected by the personalities of the two women and by the period in which each was produced. *Fifth Chinese Daughter* ⟨. . .⟩ was written for a white audience during World War II, and its popularity, to a large extent, was due to white readers' need to distinguish between friend and foe; thus, of necessity, it contains many explanations of Chinese culture and customs. Another reason for its popularity may be that it was, as critic Patricia Lin Blinde put it, "a Horatio Alger account in Chinese guise," demonstrating the greatness of America in that even a minority woman much repressed by her family could attain the American Dream. *The Woman Warrior*, an outgrowth of the Civil Rights and Women's Liberation movements of the 1960s and 1970s, is a much more personal text, written not as an exemplum for others but as a means of exorcising the personal ghosts that haunt the author. It is written for the author herself, as well as for other women, and for Chinese Americans, whom at one point she directly addresses (5–6).

Fifth Chinese Daughter is subdued in tone, polite, restrained, well-brought up ⟨. . .⟩ a sober, straightforward narrative delivered in chronological order, as though to tell this much were effort enough.

—Amy Ling, *Between Worlds: Women Writers of Chinese Ancestry* (Elmsford, NY: Pergamon Press, 1990), 119–20

SHIRLEY GEOK-LIN LIM

As artifacts of the imagination, there is little to differentiate between *Fifth Chinese Daughter*, the autobiography of Wong, who was born in the United States, and *Chinatown Family*, the novel by Lin Yutang, born in China. Both books, published around the same period, treat the myth of the cultural drive to success in immigrant Asian society, derived from the dogma of the patriarchal network in which the individual finds value through contributive work. In fact, Lin Yutang's novel remains throughout at the level of social stereotyping. ⟨. . .⟩

Wong's book, written in the third person, makes for more powerful literature. While, like Lin Yutang, she has deliberately manipulated the structure of the book so as to create opportunities to trot out all the phenomenology that forms the common opinion of Asian experience (Chinese cooking, foods, celebrations, familial duties, and so on), *Fifth Chinese Daughter* has an element of the unpredictable that challenges these stereotypes and promises every now and again to expose these racial myths. The father, a domineering patriarch, is also an ambiguous figure infected by his new country's vision of equality. The underlying drama of the daughter's challenge to her father contradicts and exceeds the given ideas of Chinese familial relationships. In confronting the limitations of popular perceptions of Chinese traits, Wong appears in some danger of offering only a reversal of attitudes. The pieties associated with Asian Americans (based on the primacy of the patriarchal family units, on obedience, and on formality of behavior) observed in conflict with white American countervalues (the importance of individuality, freedom of speech and action, and spontaneity) are unsympathetically portrayed through the point of view of the author's persona, the socially and professionally ambitious daughter.

This book, however, is more than a neat, hostile overturning of Asian pieties. Its power rests on the unconscious paradox that holds together in a larger frame the simpler narration of conflict as the daughter becomes assimilated into white American culture and therefore apparently less filial. While Chinese attitudes frustrate and demean the protagonist in her daily life, her purpose as she develops is to prove worthy of approval from her father who symbolizes Chinese patriarchal society. Unlike conventional fictions of conflict and identity, *Fifth Chinese Daughter*, although it presents the ambivalence of living in two cultures seemingly inimical to each other, does not clearly set up opposing points of view. The narrative does not contain a rejection of or an attempt to integrate the Asian paradigm to a white American model.

Finally, the author subverts her own endeavor and reveals her hidden agenda: not to rebel against her family but to compel her family to recognize and accept her. Actions lead to a reintegration of the individual *into* the Asian paradigm; the latter part of the book is a series of individual accomplishments seen as significant only insofar as they impress the patriarchal structure. The narrator-persona felt triumph at winning an essay competition run by the War Department, for example, because "this was the first occasion when the entire Wong family was assembled in pride of their fifth daughter" (198).

In the book's conclusion, the father tells his daughter of a letter he had written to a cousin long ago: "I am hoping that someday I may be able to claim that by my stand I have washed away the former disgraces suffered by the women of our family." As readers we are shocked by his self-ignorant and arrogant assertion—that he was the agent in the daughter's push for her rights—when his past actions had shown him to be reactionary. But it is even more distressing to discover that the author-narrator is herself taken in by his hypocrisy. "For the first time in her life," Wong tells us at this supreme point of paternal approval, "she felt contentment" (246). The absence of irony where it seems to be most pertinent makes *Fifth Chinese Daughter* a peculiarly Asian document. Despite the detailed expressions of conflict between the protagonist and her Chinese milieu, in her incapacity for irony Wong demonstrates the single vision in her autobiography—a vision that is unswervingly Chinese and only incidentally occidental.

 —Shirley Geok-lin Lim, "Twelve Asian American Writers: In Search of Self-Definition," *Redefining American Literary History*, ed. A. LaVonne Brown Ruoff and Jerry W. Ward, Jr. (New York: The Modern Language Association of America, 1990), 238–239

SHIRLEY GEOK-LIN LIM

In the tradition of Chinese American lifestories, *Fifth Chinese Daughter* would be considered the mother text to *Woman Warrior*. ⟨. . .⟩ Yet, on first appearance, *Fifth Chinese Daughter* seems to be the antithesis of ⟨Maxine Hong⟩ Kingston's book. Wong explains in an author's note that her use of the third person is a racial and ideological choice ⟨. . . .⟩ Significantly, Wong's second book, *No Chinese Stranger*, is written in two parts; in part 1, "To the Great Person of Father," the author again addresses herself in the third person. Part 1 ends with the literal and figurative death of the patriarch: "At thirty-six, she could no longer turn to him as head of their clan, a source of wise counsel, philosophical strength, a handy Chinese reference" (149). Part 2, consequently, is titled "First Person Singular," when, after the father's death, the narrator/author is able finally to take on her full subjectivity, and speak (write) in (as) the first person. In *The Woman Warrior* the narrator first-person is foregrounded, and the voices of female rebellion, impatience, anger, and assertiveness produce the figures of female outlaws, warriors, shamans, and storytellers. The ideological choice of speaking as a Chinese or as an American is also reflected in the authors' choices of pen names. Jade Snow Wong chose an Anglicized translation of her Chinese name, while Maxine Hong, married to an Anglo-American, adopted her Anglo husband's name. *Fifth Chinese Daughter* would appear therefore to be a Chinese text, where Kingston's flamboyant use of the first person would make *The Woman Warrior* an American text.

 Both books, however, treat the knotted theme of race, made even more difficult by the threat of male, legalistic power and shame over female sexuality. ⟨. . .⟩

 Between *Fifth Chinese Daughter* and *The Woman Warrior* is a breathtaking leap in female consciousness. The fifth Chinese daughter, struggling in her schooling in the father's strict patriarchy, escapes and does not escape his narrow definitions. The third-person separation of autobiographical subject from narrative point of view subtly reinforces this "distancing" or "muting" of female subjectivity. The narrative never escapes the logocentricism of chronological documentation. It is a life presented as always controlled by the demands of narrative "history" with its emphasis on apparent "objectivity," "facticity," "chronological ordering," "the third-person point of view." *The Woman Warrior*, however, is an "over-writing" of given Chinese-Americans stories. In this attempt to "over-write," all stories are equal, whether from history, myth, legend, family lore, or individual invention. The first person dominates, and in overflowing female terms. Thus the book is replete with nouns and pronouns referring strictly to female gender: mother, aunt, she, girl babies, etc. More significantly, the presence of mother, aunts, and daughter places it in a woman-gendered tradition, whereas the constructing/constraining pole of the normative and Confucianist patriarchy locates *Fifth Chinese Daughter* in a male-constituted society. The daughter in Wong's autobiography defines herself against and through negotiations with the other gender; she is above all the patriarch's daughter. On the other hand, the presence of the daughter's discourse in *The Woman Warrior* is a "talking-back-to" the mother culture, which is also the racial culture. The appropriation of the mother's talk-stories, the conversion of oral to writerly tradition, is both the American daughter's reclamation of her Chinese mother's story (history) and her vanquishing of it, swallowing of it into her American presence (present). Logocentricism is repeatedly shattered; in its place are what appear to be fragments, of stories, ideas, thoughts, images, asides, which circle around and accumulate to form the expression of the idea of Chinese American female subjectivity.

The Woman Warrior, therefore, unlike *Fifth Chinese Daughter*, has not an autobiographical story to tell but a racial and gendered consciousness to intimate and create. It shares with another contemporary Asian American woman's text, ⟨Joy Kogawa's⟩ *Obasan*, in interrogating identities and reconstituting in their place an emergent daughterly subject, just as *Fifth Chinese Daughter* shares with Sone's *Nisei Daughter* an earlier generation's submergent subjectivities and eventual submission to patriarchal discourse. The differences between the two books are arguably differences of generational thematics; read together, *Fifth Chinese Daughter* and *The Woman Warrior* deepen each other's cultural constructions of Chinese American daughters, moving from any kind of single or singly divided consciousness to an expression of multiple subjectivities, the consequence of American daughters resignifying their Asian origins.

—Shirley Geok-lin Lim, "The Tradition of Chinese American Women's Life Stories: Thematics of Race and Gender in Jade Snow Wong's *Fifth Chinese Daughter* and Maxine Hong Kingston's *The Woman Warrior*," *American Women's Autobiography: Fea(s)ts of Memory*, ed. Margo Culley (Madison, WI: University of Wisconsin Press, 1992), 256–57, 263–64

BIBLIOGRAPHY

Fifth Chinese Daughter. 1945.
No Chinese Stranger. 1975.

Hisaye Yamamoto

b. 1921

HISAYE YAMAMOTO was born in Redondo Beach, California, in 1921, the daughter of Japanese immigrant parents. During World War II she was interned at a camp in Poston, Arizona. Yamamoto began writing in her teens and sharpened her skills during her three years of internment, serving as a reporter and columnist for the *Poston Chronicle*. There she also published her first fiction piece, a serialized mystery entitled "Death Rides the Rails to Poston."

In spite of pervasive anti-Japanese sentiment in America after the war, Yamamoto gained national recognition for her writing and was awarded a John Hay Whitney Foundation Opportunity Fellowship. From 1945 to 1955, she was a reporter for the *Los Angeles Tribune*, an African-American weekly newspaper, while at the same time publishing short stories in literary and mainstream magazines as well as in Japanese- and Asian-American publications. One of the best known female nisei (second-generation Japanese-American) writers, she has been compared by scholar King-Kok Cheung to author Henry Miller in how she dramatizes social relationships between the New World and the Old.

Among Yamamoto's most popular and haunting short stories are "Seventeen Syllables," which became the title story for her first published collection, and "Yoneko's Earthquake," which was included in *Best American Short Stories of 1952*. These two stories were also merged into a single narrative in *Hot Summer Winds*, a one-hour American Playhouse drama produced by PBS in May 1991. "Las Vegas Charley," "The Legend of Miss Sasagawara," "The Brown House," and many of her other stories have been widely anthologized and studied.

In 1986 the Before Columbus Foundation presented Yamamoto with the American Book Award for Lifetime Achievement. She is married to Anthony De Soto, with whom she has had five children, and lives in Los Angeles.

CRITICAL EXTRACTS

YURI KAGEYAMA

Despite the clear emphasis on Asian American in her work, Yamamoto, when asked if her intended audience had been other Nisei, answers that she had not been conscious of any audience when she wrote. She just wanted to get published, she says. ⟨. . .⟩

⟨. . .⟩ Yamamoto knows that Nisei writers are being dug up by the Sansei, with their newly awakened "Japanese American identity" (as a result of the Civil Rights and 60's non-white movements), who are enthusiastic to reclaim their cultural heritage. She seems almost embarrassed that, after years of solitary struggle as a relatively obscure writer, she is now being elevated to the peculiar position of cult leader or some embodiment of ethnic history and culture.

It was natural for her to write about being Nisei, for that is what she is, just as it was natural for her to write about being a woman or a Christian. This writer used to believe that the unwillingness of Yamamoto and other Nisei writers to assert more aggressively a brand of cultural nationalism or some such anti-racist and pro-ethnic ideology was a weakness. But, upon closer examination, it became increasingly clear that the "Japanese American-ness" expressed in Nissei (and Issei) art forms is far superior—that is, more genuine precisely because of their naturalness—to those propagandistic works by many Sansei that are supposed to be so "Japanese American" and "politically progressive," but are, in fact, forced rhetoric and, therefore, in a sense, dishonest.

In other words, unlike Yamamoto's characters, who live and breathe as true people, the "community" which appears in much of Sansei "political" literature are either ghosts of Issei grandparents they could never communicate with (due to the language barrier) and usually interned Nisei, or else abstractions of some "activist" clique which remains in our ghettos, mostly through bureaucratized social service agencies. The stronger Sansei works are inevitably those that deal honestly with their own experiences (including the *Sansei* perceptions of Issei or Nisei, as well as of themselves)—which is a complex contradiction for the Sansei, whose ethnic group has largely dispersed geographically and are, to a large extent, busily working at assimilating (if not at quiet genocide through inter-marriage).

The lesson that the Sansei has to learn from writers like Hisaye Yamamoto should not be a zealous idealization of the Nisei (or Issei) "roots." Instead, the inspiration is that: the potency of Yamamoto's works—as with all great literature—lies in her writing, not only with a technical craftsmanship, but also, more significantly, with truthfulness and integrity.

—Yuri Kageyama, "Hisaye Yamamoto—Nisei Writer," *Sunbury* 10 (1981): 39–41

STAN YOGI

Yamamoto's stories are not only powerful portraits of Japanese American life, they are also technically fascinating. Through the use of narrators with limited perspectives, Yamamoto develops "buried plots," veiled means of conveying stories that link her work with feminist critical theory as well as with Japanese American communication patterns. Yamamoto crafts stories with surface meanings that hint at powerful undercurrents. In uncovering the buried plots of Yamamoto's stories, one can not only better understand the experiences of Japanese Americans but also explore the intersection of gender, culture, and language. ⟨. . .⟩

"Seventeen Syllables" operates on a series of deceptions and opens with an innocent hoax. After Mrs. Hayashi recites a haiku she has composed in Japanese, Rosie pretends "to understand it thoroughly and appreciate it no end" ⟨8⟩. Although Mrs. Hayashi seeks to convey the beauty of her hobby, an absence of genuine communication between the two women occurs because Rosie does not understand the Japanese her mother uses. For Rosie, "it was so much easier to say, yes, yes even when one meant no, no" (8), and she innocently attempts to deceive her mother by pretending to enjoy the poem.

Yamamoto links this initial and innocent deception to more calculated trickery. Jesus Carrasco, the son of seasonal workers, invites Rosie to meet him in a packing shed because, he tells Rosie, "I've got a secret I want to tell you." The two youths engage in adolescent teasing, and from this context it becomes apparent that Jesus' "secret" is a pretense to meet Rosie alone. Rosie, however, is blind to the import of Jesus' invitation. When she arrives at the shed at the appointed time she demands "now tell me the secret."

Jesus' claim of conveying a secret is not completely without merit, for he proceeds to disclose to Rosie what was, up to this point in her life, a secret: the complexity of sexual attraction. In her encounter with Jesus, Rosie echoes her earlier response to her mother:

> When he took hold of her empty hand, she could find no words to
> protest; her vocabulary had become distressingly constricted and she
> thought desperately that all that remained intact now was yes and no
> and oh, and even these few sounds would not easily out. Thus, kissed
> by Jesus, Rosie fell for the first time entirely victim to a helplessness
> delectable beyond speech (14).

This image of Rosie, utterly dumfounded, strikingly resembles her struggle to hide her ignorance of the haiku's meaning. In her experience with Jesus, however, the limited vocabulary of "yes" and "no" reappears but cannot even be vocalized; Jesus has left her speechless. With the realization that "yes" and "no" are the basic words through which individuals express their will, one begins to recognize an important link between Rosie's encounter with Jesus and her earlier experience with her mother. For Mrs. Hayashi, writing haiku is a means of asserting herself and escaping the daily toil on the farm. Rosie's loss of will in this situation thus becomes an innocent analogue to the control Mrs.

Hayashi lacks over her own life. Much like Rosie, who succumbs to Jesus' desires, Mrs. Hayashi is forced to cease writing by her husband.

Once establishing the plot concerning Rosie's relationship with Jesus, Yamamoto begins to develop the buried plot regarding Mrs. Hayashi. Jesus' deception of Rosie, resulting in her initiation into sexual knowledge, is in turn linked to the confession of deception that Rosie's mother makes. After serenely observing her husband chop up and burn the prize she won in a haiku contest, Mrs. Hayashi narrates the history behind her immigration to the U.S., a history hitherto kept secret:

> At eighteen she had been in love with the first son of one of the well-to-do families in her village. The two had met whenever and wherever they could, secretly, because it would not have done for his family to see him favor her—her father had no money; he was a drunkard and a gambler besides. She had learned she was with child; an excellent match had already been arranged for her lover. Despised by her family, she had given premature birth to a stillborn son, who would be seventeen now (18).

As an alternative to suicide, Mrs. Hayashi asks her sister in America to send for her. Her sister arranges a marriage with Rosie's father, who "was never told why his unseen betrothed was so eager to hasten the day of meeting" (19).

Mrs. Hayashi's confession brings together many of the themes already introduced in the story. The constriction of communication explored in the opening has its more tragic parallel in the experiences of Rosie's mother: Mrs. Hayashi has no means of expressing her desires and feelings other than to kill herself or run away. She cannot, moreover, reveal her tarnished past to her husband. The theme of blossoming sexuality has its more dire consequences for Mrs. Hayashi. She consummates her affair but has no power to make it binding. Others dictate the termination of her relationship, and the stillborn child serves as a manifestation of her lost love. Although Mrs. Hayashi's arranged marriage is not too far from common practice, her case is burdened with complicating circumstances: her family ships her off in shame, and she hides the secret of her affair and dead child from her husband. The options open to her are few. Having severed family ties, she cannot return to Japan. She is trapped in America, where she works like a machine in the fields and packing sheds. Writing, one of the few escapes from her demanding life, is denied her. Just as her love affair is cut off, just as her son is born too soon, so too is her career as a poet prematurely halted.

Only after learning of Mrs. Hayashi's history are the implications of the title "Seventeen Syllables" fleshed out. The haikus that Rosie's mother writes become metaphors of both freedom and constraint. Writing allows Mrs.

Hayashi to transcend her mundane and harsh existence and ponder higher ideas. The haiku form, in which "she must pack all her meaning into seventeen syllables," also becomes a metaphor for the constraints that force Mrs. Hayashi to find meaning in small ways. The number seventeen, in addition, has special meaning for both Rosie and her mother. For Mrs. Hayashi, the number recalls a tragic loss; her stillborn son would at the time of the story be seventeen years old. For Rosie, however, the number carries tremendous hope. Jesus, soon to be a senior in high school and her guide to budding sexuality, is probably seventeen years old.

—Stan Yogi, "Legacies Revealed: Uncovering Buried Plots in the Stories of Hisaye Yamamoto," *Studies in American Fiction* 17, no. 2 (Autumn 1989): 170–72

KING-KOK CHEUNG

Yamamoto's literary acclaim derives in part from her consummate narrative strategies. Her technique of double-telling—conveying two tales in the guise of one—involves an intertextual use of a familiar device. In two of her most haunting stories, "Seventeen Syllables" and "Yoneko's Earthquake," the overt "action" is presented through a naive narrator who reflects the mind of a young girl, while the covert drama concerns the conflict between the girl's issei (first-generation) parents. Though undoubtedly influenced by modernist experimentation with limited point of view, Yamamoto tailors the method to the Japanese American context. Her two stories capitalize not only on the infrequent verbal communication between issei spouses but also on the peculiar interaction between issei parents and nisei children. Issei parents (especially fathers) tend to be authoritative and protective toward the young, so that free verbal exchange between parents and children is frequently suppressed. By playing the naive nisei point of view against the pregnant silence of the issei, Yamamoto constructs hidden plots and deflects attention from unsettling messages. Suspense develops in both stories in part because the parents refrain from disclosing adult problems to their children; only through the ingenuous telling of the nisei daughters do we catch the dark nuances of adult reticence. ⟨. . .⟩

What ⟨Elaine⟩ Showalter calls "double-voiced discourse" certainly informs these two stories, in which the muted sufferings of the mothers emerge belatedly. But Yamamoto's plots also monitor male silences. If mothers and daughters in the two stories often talk at cross-purposes, communication between fathers and daughters is altogether restricted. In the few instances in which the fathers do speak, the tone is generally peremptory or critical. Interaction between the spouses is scarcely better. Yet the tight-lipped husbands, ostensibly "guardians of the prison doors" ⟨Elaine Kim, "Defining Asian American Realities Through Literature," 99⟩, are themselves bound by patriarchal conventions. ⟨. . .⟩

The fathers' stories are told even more indirectly than the mothers'. Where the subjective responses of the daughters often reflect the mothers' hidden passions, only the daughters' offhand observations suggest the fathers' woes. Nevertheless, both narratives are punctuated with sufficient hints to indicate that mounting masculine anxiety, not habitual insensitivity, sparks violence. The seemingly impassive Mr. Hayashi may in fact be plagued by loneliness, inadequacy, and jealousy, though none of these feelings have been openly admitted by the character or noted by the narrator. The narrator does mention, however, that Mr. Hayashi and his wife used to play cards together before retiring jointly and that as a result of Mrs. Hayashi's new interest, he has to "resort to solitaire" (9). Since Mrs. Hayashi composes late into the night, we may further assume that her husband now goes to bed alone. His annoyance during the visit to the Hayanos obviously emanates from his feeling excluded from the intellectual discussion. But the reader may deduce jealousy as an additional provocation. Mr. Hayano, whose wife has already lost both health and beauty, is himself "handsome, tall, and strong" (10), at least in Rosie's eyes. Buzzing through the elisions is the suggestion that not fatigue (the reason voiced by Mrs. Hayashi) but jealousy drives Mr. Hayashi away. Mrs. Hayashi's former lover was a man from a higher social class; Mr. Hayashi—a farmer—came from a class lower than that of his wife's family. He may feel troubled by Mrs. Hayashi's verbal sophistication, itself a reminder of their disparate class origins. Above all, he may sense a compatibility or suspect a bond—physical and intellectual—between his wife and Mr. Hayano that is absent in either of the marriages.

Mr. Hosoume's behavior suggests also that his male pride is chafed by an unspeakable cause—his sexual impotence. Out of his own sense of injured manhood he grumbles about his children's disrespect, slaps his wife for contradicting him, and threatens to fire Marpo for interfering. Furthermore, he links everyone's "impudent" behavior to his "illness" (54), betraying an obsessive anxiety. Given that he thinks his family is turning against him out of scorn, his wife's love affair and ensuing pregnancy must be an ultimate affront to his masculine image. His aggression on the way to the hospital can be better understood in the light of his mortification: the fetus is an irksome reminder at once of cuckoldry and impotence. ⟨. . .⟩

To mitigate the initial negative impressions of Mr. Hayashi and Mr. Hosoume is not to condone their actions but to show that their behavior deserves more sympathetic analysis than dismissal as the general "failure of the [issei] fathers" ⟨Charles Crow, "*Issei* Father," 1986, 34⟩. Had the fathers been able to reveal their vulnerability, the tragic endings might have been averted; instead they *gaman* till their escalated anger erupts in violence. Meanwhile, their taciturnity may have widened the gap between themselves and their spouses, who not surprisingly become drawn to the likes of Mr. Hayano, Mr. Kuroda, and Marpo; physical and intellectual attractions aside, these men communicate verbally with the women.

The two stories may have encoded Yamamoto's own ambivalence toward her cultural inheritance. Her use of native narrators embodying the free spirits of the young nisei sets off the rigid conventions that riddle the lives of issei women and men. Seen through the startled or uncomprehending eyes of bicultural daughters who must soon come to grips with their maternal legacies, the mothers' private sorrow and the fathers' brooding rage reverberate ominously. On the other hand, Yamamoto's stylistic restraint pays a tacit tribute to those cultural forerunners who can say more in less, who can funnel vast meaning and feeling into seventeen syllables. Here strategy of double-telling is especially suited to evoking suppressed feelings, revealing the anxieties and hurts that lie beneath the surface of language. The hushed climax of each story is captured in a verbal snapshot: by zooming in on the deliberate destruction of the Hiroshige and on the steady crushing of the collie, she transmits and trans-mutes the characters' unspoken emotions through her own articulate silence.

—King-Kok Cheung, "Double-Telling: Intertextual Silence in Hisaye Yamamoto's Fiction," *American Literary History* 3, no. 2 (Summer 1991): 278, 288, 290–92

KING-KOK CHEUNG

Fredric Jameson notes that Third World texts, no matter how private they seem, "necessarily project a political dimension in the form of a national allegory: the story of the private individual is always an allegory of the embattled situation of the public third-world culture and society" ⟨"Third-World Literature in the Era of Multinational Capitalism," 1986, 69⟩. His observation applies with peculiar force to "The Legend." The politics of the time not only contributes directly to Miss Sasagawara's distress but also figures directly as the allegorical level of the story. Within the individual story, the congestion at camp intensifies the gaze on Miss Sasagawara and accelerates the spreading of gossip. As an allegory the scandal-loving and finger-pointing community has a counterpart in the white majority that allowed themselves to be swayed by prejudice and hearsay into endorsing the imprisonment of an entire people. In an essay in which Yamamoto refers briefly to "The Legend," she writes:

> Anthologists of this story have commented, "The author is far less concerned with the social significance of the external environment than with the internal state of the characters," and asked, "Is Miss Sasagawara insane or are those who accept the life of the camps insane?" (". . . I Still Carry It Around" 15)

That Yamamoto has chosen to highlight those two points made by commentators is instructive. Their first observation is, I believe, belied by the answer(s)
to their second question—a narrative crux that connects the "internal state" to
the "external environment" and glues together the realistic and the allegorical
dimensions of "The Legend." Just as the rumors about Miss Sasagawara accord
well with the stereotypes of dancer or spinster, much of the incriminating "evidence" leading to persecution conformed to the ruling culture's historical prejudice against people of Japanese descent. Elsie's questionable reading of Miss
Sasagawara's vacant expression and Mrs. Sasaki's dubious inference have parallels in the many official misinterpretations of *nikkei* activities, misinterpretations which built up into what Ronald Takaki calls "the myth of 'military
necessity' for Japanese-American internment" ⟨*Strangers from a Different Shore,*
1989, 379⟩. ⟨. . .⟩

While I am not arguing for any simple correspondences between the
rumors enveloping the dancer and those hovering over *nikkei* at large, I believe
that the story goes well beyond an individual tragedy and that the many indirect political allusions in "The Legend" press us to reinterpret the "reports"
associated with Miss Sasagawara. Her hypersensitivity to being spied upon
not only mirrors the wartime hysteria and paranoia of the white majority but
also reflects back on the plight of her own ethnic group. Her visibility and susceptibility to scrutiny bespeak the *nikkei* predicament during World War II,
which drastically sharpened the external gaze on this Asian minority. The
communal assumption of Miss Sasagawara's pathology echoes the government's speculation that many *nikkei* residing on the West Coast could be devi-
ous spies. The isolation and eventual institutionalization of Miss Sasagawara
correspond to the exclusion and ultimate detention of the race.

—King-Kok Cheung, "Thrice Muted Tale: Interplay of Art and Politics in Hisaye Yamamoto's 'The Legend of Miss Sasagawara,'" *MELUS* 17, no. 3 (Fall 1991–92): 116–18

ROBERT M. PAYNE

Because Yamamoto's young main characters are not aware of all the important
events influencing their lives, the reader of both "Yoneko's Earthquake" and
"Seventeen Syllables" must peer beyond the girls' limited purview to discern
the narratives' crucial hidden content. Abandoning seamless narrative closure,
Yamamoto crafts a writerly text that demands the participation of her audience
to complement the written story with their own construction of the absent
narrative.

Perhaps inspired by the evocative understatement of haiku, Yamamoto's
narrative strategy calls attention to the ethnic issues inherent to her stories.
Her characters' status as so-called ethnic minorities suggests a problematic
relationship to their own Americanness: straddling but separated from the sig-

nifiers of two cultures, Japanese and American, the *issei* and *nisei* characters are crucibles of a new identity which must discover its own meaning and purpose. As personified by Yoneko, a Japanese American identity already exists, but it is still unfinished, growing, maturing. However, rather than unproblematically defining a "Japanese American" identity, Yamamoto's synthesis of disparate cultural signifiers ultimately turns in on itself: the constant exchange of culturally distinctive ideas and activities among the diverse characters implicitly questions the narrow idea of culture as a collection of fixed, insular ethnic groups. Furthermore, the possibility, however deferred, of intercultural/ interethnic unions in Yamamoto's stories also indicates—and perhaps celebrates—the constantly fluctuating cultural and ethnic makeup of America's human landscape. Yoneko may exemplify a synthesis of Japanese and American cultures, but she can't contain the boundless fluidity of cultural interaction.

In this context, Yamamoto's narrative ellipses take on an added resonance. Discussing the ambivalence of both narration and the national self-image, Homi K. Bhabha connects the loose-ended narrative to resistance against the nation's narrative authority and its construction of an unquestioned, seemingly homogeneous national identity ⟨. . . .⟩

The reader, then, may easily interpret Yamamoto's crucial narrative absences as a correlation to the relative absence of Japanese Americans—and people of color in general—in the discourse of American history as it has traditionally been taught in mainstream education. In particular, the pedagogical absence of the Japanese American internment, only recently remedied, has long elided this crucial event in the history of the U.S. constitution. Also, Yamamoto's narrative lacunae are associable to invisibly oppressive power relations among the characters in her stories: the absence of important narrative information marks the missing alternative voice of the underling. Just as they suggest the amorphous space of an alternate literary discourse, the rupturous gaps in Yamamoto's stories suggest the contours of a perceptually radical history denied by patriarchy, hierarchy, and racism. By drawing the reader to the silences *within* the open-ended narrative, Yamamoto's stories quietly question what remains to be said *beyond* the narrative, and beyond the construct of American culture as fundamentally immutable and Eurocentric.

—Robert M. Payne, "Adapting (to) the Margins: *Hot Summer Winds* and the Stories of Hisaye Yamamoto," *East-West Film Journal* 7, no. 2 (July 1993): 42–43

WILLIAM P. OSBORN AND SYLVIA A. WATANABE

⟨Osborn/Watanabe:⟩ In a recent issue of *The Northwest Nikkei Review*, you responded pretty vigorously to the question, "Do publishers discriminate against Asian males?"

⟨Yamamoto:⟩ Well, I don't think that the implicit charge was valid at all. David Mura and Garett Hongo are being published, you know, and Frank Chin has several books coming out in a row. I guess what they mean is the best sellers like Amy Tan and Maxine Hong Kingston—that there hasn't been an Asian-American male writer who's got the same acclaim, yes? Hm. Well, I guess they should just wait. Their turn will come. Because they all write well, the ones who've been published.

⟨Osborn/Watanabe:⟩ What do you think of the stand taken by some other Asian-American writers, that priority must be given to developing an Asian-American readership?

⟨Yamamoto:⟩ I guess I'm just writing to please myself, express myself, mainly, since I don't know anybody's ever going to read it. I'm just trying to put down whatever is stuck in my craw as best I can. You know, get it out of my system. I've never thought of writing *for* anybody. I don't think you can write aiming at a specifically Asian-American audience if you want to write freely. No, you just express yourself without thinking of that angle. I think more and more Asian-American writers will be doing that, you know—like this sansei generation. Cynthia Kadohata—the fact that she's sansei doesn't figure that importantly. She might mention the Asian-American background in passing, but that's not the main thrust of her work.

⟨Osborn/Watanabe:⟩ That seems related to the point made by Bharati Mukherjee at a recent reading at the University of Michigan. She said that though she writes from her experience as an Asian-American, she would like to be thought of as an *American* writer. How do you see yourself—how would you like to be seen?

⟨Yamamoto:⟩ I don't even bother to tell people I'm Japanese-American anymore, because that's not what they want to know. I just say I'm Japanese. Not pridefully or anything, just a statement of fact. Of course I don't care for generalizations about any race. I know there will always be those who see the Asian in me first. But I go to the supermarket, the dentist, the malls, the museums, etc., without thinking about others' attitudes about me and so far haven't felt any particular hostility. But yes, I think any writer would like to be generally accepted and not just on his or her own ethnic background. People don't say of Saul Bellow or Philip Roth, I'm going to read this Jewish writer, you know. So, well, I think it's okay to want to be generally accepted. But it's the general public that decides. Some will read my work because they consider it a valid part of American literature, or some will read it because it's about a specific ethnic background. Look at Amy Tan—wasn't she thirty-some weeks on the best seller list? And it wasn't just Chinese-Americans reading her. Everybody was. She will be studied as an ethnic writer, but some obviously won't be bound by that.

—William P. Osborn and Sylvia A. Watanabe, "A Conversation with Hisaye Yamamoto," *Chicago Review* 39, nos. 3 and 4 (Summer/Fall 1993): 35–36

MING L. CHENG

Examination of "Seventeen Syllables" in the context of gender, economic, and social limitations yields a more complete understanding of the complexities of Yamamoto's characters ⟨than has recent criticism that has largely ignored the male perspective⟩. In the analysis of human actions bound by external limitations, there are those actions motivated by necessity, and the counterbalancing actions motivated by extravagance. In Yamamoto's works, more often necessity is the domain of the male, while extravagance is the realm of the female. But the importance which should not be lost is that all characters, male or female, are subject to the social and economic limitations of the macrocosm, and the traditional and gender limitations of the microcosm. It is through examination of these limitations that we can come to a more complete understanding of the ulterior causation of a character's thoughts and actions. ⟨. . .⟩

The thwarting of extravagance by necessity is a common thread binding "Seventeen Syllables" to two of Yamamoto's other works, "Yoneko's Earthquake" and "Miss Sasagawara." "Yoneko's Earthquake," published two years later, contains much of the same plot dynamics and symbolism. There is the initial exercise of authority by the male when Mr. Hosoume, in disciplining his wife, draws a line justified by necessity. Similarly, as Yoneko's mother delves deeper into extravagance, Yoneko follows. Mrs. Hosoume subsequently engages in an extravagant, an illicit affair—clearly crossing the line, forcing the second, violent act of authority: the abortion and the departure of Marpo, the hired hand and Mrs. Hosoume's lover. Unlike "Seventeen Syllables," Mrs. Hosoume's extravagance, embodied in her aborted fetus, is fruitless, as Yoneko, devastated and emotionally drained by Marpo's departure, rejects extravagance. "The Legend of Miss Sasagawara" is narrated by Kiku, whose internment in an Arizona camp is punctuated by the intrigue surrounding a female camp member. Camp crowding blurs personal and public life, creating a pressure to conform or risk ridicule. Into this setting is thrust the dancer Mari and her father Rev. Sasagawara, an ascetic with whom she must share living quarters. While her father epitomizes the extremes of necessity required for sainthood, the incompatibility of his devotion with Mari's extravagance, "passions rising, subsiding, and again rising, perhaps in anguished silence, within the selfsame room," leads her to describe her father's saintly devotion as madness—yet it is her extravagance which is derided by the camp as madness (33). For Miss Sasagawara, an artist previously free to dance unshackled by necessity, the limitations imposed by her macrocosm are severe. In Mari's realm, the realm of the lyrical and the romantic, of the extravagance of ballet, it is not extravagance but ascetic necessity which is "madness, the monstrous sort which, pure of itself, might possibly bring troublous, scented scenes to recur in the other's sleep" (33).

In the context of external and internal limitations, limited points of view and secondary plots are revealed to be not mere literary devices but artful brushstrokes upon a much larger canvas. If a singer imparts by the arch in her back and the strain in her neck more than what her words themselves can say, then Yamamoto conveys through her unreliable narrators the painful effects of human limitations to greater effect than her plots do tell. Mrs. Hosoume's affair is more passionate than Ume Hanazono's flirtation with haiku, and the death of collie and unborn child is more violent and repulsive than the destruction of the Hiroshiges. The resulting psychological trauma borne by Yoneko, and the limitations of her narration, is correspondingly much greater than that of Rosie—even the title is suggestive of the greater depth of anguish Yoneko has experienced. Similarly, while the internees in Kuki's camp experience dehumanization, their denial and concomitant rejection of Miss Sasagawara's extravagance are balms which soothe their pain. In "Seventeen Syllables," as in "Yoneko's Earthquake" and "Miss Sasagawara," the narrative is composed by a reluctant witness whose life has been leveled, in Rosie's own words, "to the very ground" (18). In recounting a deep wound in her psyche, it is at once inevitable and revealing that Rosie is unreliable—for what is not told is often as meaningful as what is. Denial and a limited point of view allow Rosie, and Yoneko and Kuki as well, to cope with childhoods scarred by the violent effects of external limitations. Despite the pain, however, for Rosie, the least scarred of these three children, there is yet hope. Although Rosie's mother laments her daughter's inability to understand her message, it is not evident that Rosie does not. Rosie, the seed of her mother, may yet burst forth in the passionate flame of vindication.

—Ming L. Cheng, "The Unrepentant Fire: Tragic Limitations in Hisaye Yamamoto's 'Seventeen Syllables,'" *MELUS* 19, no. 4 (Winter 1994): 102–4

BIBLIOGRAPHY

Seventeen Syllables: Five Stories of Japanese American Life (published in Tokyo). 1985.
Seventeen Syllables and Other Stories. 1988.
Hot Summer Winds (screenplay). 1988.

Wakako Yamauchi

b. 1924

WAKAKO YAMAUCHI was born on or just before October 25, 1924, in Westmorland, California, to Yasaku Nakamura and Hamako Machida, immigrant tenant farmers. Not eligible for citizenship and forbidden to own property under California's Alien Land Law, her parents moved the family every few years in order to find work. In the mid-1930s, their nomadic existence came to an end when they settled in Oceanside, California, to run a boarding house for Japanese immigrants. But the order of their new life was interrupted by the outbreak of World War II during Wakako's senior year of high school.

Throughout the war the family was interned at a relocation camp in Poston, Arizona, where Wakako found work as a layout artist at the *Poston Chronicle*, the camp newspaper. There she met fellow writer Hisaye Yamamoto, a few years her senior and already becoming established in the Japanese-American press. Wakako followed Yamamoto around the camp while she took notes for her column in the *Chronicle*, but what began as veneration and mentoring soon transformed into a friendship of mutual inspiration and artistic support.

Released early from camp in 1944 by signing a "loyalty oath," Wakako moved to Chicago, where she worked for a candy factory until 1945, when she rejoined her mother and siblings in San Diego. Barely a year later, she moved to Los Angeles, where she roomed with Hisaye Yamamoto and took classes in drawing, layout, and painting at the Otis Art Center. In 1948, she married Chester Yamauchi, with whom she subsequently had one daughter, Joy. From 1960 to 1974, she published one drawing and one story a year in the Japanese-American daily, *Los Angeles Rafu Shimpo*, though by her own account she was primarily a housewife and mother. One early story, "And the Soul Shall Dance," was printed in the Asian-American anthology *Aiiieeeee!* in 1974, bringing Yamauchi greater recognition. Divorced in 1975, she began writing full time.

She completed her first play, *And the Soul Shall Dance* (based on the short story) in 1976 with a Rockefeller playwright-in-residence grant. The two-act drama recreates the environment of California's Imperial Valley during the 1930s, focusing on the lives of two Japanese-American families struggling to survive as farmers. Yamauchi uses this setting to mesh complex themes: racism, assimilation, identity, sexual awakening, coming of age, rebellion against proscribed gender and generational structures. The play was originally staged by the East-

West players, a mostly Asian-American theater group in Los Angeles, and it was nominated for Outstanding New Play of the Year by the Los Angeles Drama Critics Circle. Hollywood Television Theatre produced a teleplay version broadcast nationally on the Arts and Entertainment Channel and on PBS.

Considered pioneering work of Asian-American drama, Yamauchi's plays have been staged at theaters across the country. Art, music, and culture play an important role in the lives of her characters throughout her writing, which deals with the timeless conflicts of relationships amidst the barriers of race and class discrimination. In addition to writing plays, Yamauchi continues to write short stories and essays, which are widely published in literary, academic, and Japanese-American publications. A substantial selection of her work has been published in *Songs My Mother Taught Me: Stories, Plays, and Memoir*.

Yamauchi has received numerous awards and fellowships, including several Rockefeller grants, the Brody Art Fund Fellowship, and the American Theater Critics Regional Award for Outstanding Play. She lives in Gardena, California.

CRITICAL EXTRACTS

JANICE ARKATOV

Originally inspired by a "face box" (an eerie souvenir she acquired in Hawaii several years ago), "Memento" is the story ⟨of, describes Yamauchi,⟩ two women, who as girls battled over the same man. Now, 30 years later, the one who got the man returns—as a widow—to offer the memento to her old girlfriend. And as she puts it on, a story unfolds.

"It could be a psychodrama—in her mind—or it could be, if you believe in such things, a curse," the playwright continued vaguely. "So the rest of the play could be fantasies or actualities. The women continue in the action, as themselves and as other people.

"This was a story first," Yamauchi stressed. In fact, all of her plays began life as short stories. It's a form she often returns to: "When I get stuck in a play, I go back and write a short story, so I can see the motion, the movement—the thrust of it. If you can just write it simply as a short story, it's much easier to develop. And, you know, a short story is most like a play (in terms of writing styles) in that it's clean and taut and there's no dawdling.

"Of course, there are differences. In a play, you have to show with dialogue how a person feels; in a story you can just say 'He was angry.' In a play, the anger would have to be coming out of his mouth, expressed in words and action." ⟨. . .⟩

The cultural basis in her work, she pointed out, is merely a by-product of her original intent: "I wanted to be *honest*, write about what I knew." And since she lived through the internment camps of World War II (she was in her late teens when her family was relocated and incarcerated in Arizona), she often returns—in her work—to that experience.

Yamauchi does not consider her attention to the subject either morbid or limiting.

"Sure, it's painful to remember," she nodded. "I think you can distance yourself from it (in life), but the work has to include it. It's part of what made me what I am, what makes me think the way I do." She acknowledges that her concerns are probably more personal than civic-minded. "Maybe it's just for myself that I do this. I want to talk about my mother, my father, my sisters and brothers. They don't always know they're in my plays, but they are."

—Janice Arkatov, "The Soul and the Playwright Shall Dance," *The Los Angeles Times* (8 February 1986): V-3

STAN YOGI

Some of the best and most well-known short stories of Wakako Yamauchi and Hisaye Yamamoto explore how the aspirations of Issei (Japanese immigrant) women collide with the patriarchal norms of Issei culture. Yamauchi's "And the Soul Shall Dance" (1966) and "Songs My Mother Taught Me" (1976) and Yamamoto's "Seventeen Syllables" (1949) and "Yoneko's Earthquake" (1951) depict Issei women striving to realize ambitions that contradict traditional roles. Although marriage afforded Issei men greater control over their lives, for Issei women it meant the transference of obedience from parents to husband. An Issei woman's primary concern was to provide for the well-being of her family. In this context, Issei women's efforts at self-fulfillment outside the boundaries of family and community necessarily become rebellions against cultural standards.

Yamauchi and Yamamoto portray the resistance of Issei women and the consequences of their rebellions in narratives that subvert the strict cultural codes of the Issei family. Told from the perspectives of Nisei (second-generation Japanese American) daughters who view their mothers sympathetically, the narratives temper empathy with objectivity; if the Issei women themselves narrated the stories, melodrama or self-pity could dominate the narratives. Through the first-person narrators who selectively reveal informa-

tion in the stories of Yamauchi or through the third-person narrators with limited perspectives in the stories of Yamamoto, readers discover the Issei
women's defiance in much the same way as do the daughters who observe their
mothers: through indirect actions and perceptions that often defy definitive
explication. These narratives thus not only quietly subvert the rigid constructs
of the Issei family by portraying sympathetically such taboo behavior as
women's drunkenness and adultery, they also subtly suggest, through the reactions of Nisei daughters to their mothers, the transformation of the very standards the mothers violate.

Of the four stories, Yamauchi's "And the Soul Shall Dance" is the most
straightforward in its presentation of an Issei woman's rebellion. The reminiscence of a Nisei named Masako, the story depicts her childhood fascination
with Mrs. Oka, an aloof, disturbed Issei neighbor whose unconventional
behavior is both frightening and intriguing. Mrs. Oka, though, is not the only
unhappy woman in the story. Through the complex relationships among the
four female characters, Yamauchi depicts both resistance and containment
among Issei and Nisei women.

Mrs. Oka is the most visibly agitated character. An arranged marriage with
her dead sister's husband sparks her frustration. Although Mrs. Oka's marriage
does not diverge radically from Japanese custom, it keenly underscores her
powerlessness. She does not control her destiny and is coerced into marriage
and shipped off to lead a harsh farm life. That she would not defy the marriage
may strike readers as odd. The options open to Issei women, however, were few.
As Yuji Ichioka points out, "To refuse [a picture-marriage] would have been an
act of filial disobedience, a grave moral offense" ⟨The Issei, 1988, 166⟩. In addition, once in the United States, Issei women, lacking English-language skills
and ignorant of their new environments, were dependent on their husbands.

Mrs. Oka does, however, register her unhappiness by drinking, a habit
uncommon among Issei women. As Masako comments, Mrs. Oka's "aberration
was a protest of the life assigned her" (196). This protest, although "obstinate,"
is "unobserved" and "unheeded" (196). The denial of Mrs. Oka's behavior not
only reflects the discomfort of confronting disturbing actions, it also becomes
a de facto means of punishing her for protesting her circumstances.
Consequently, she further distances herself to a point where displaying the
"welts and bruises on her usually smooth brown face" (194)—the results of
brawls with her husband—becomes a form of resistance; the injuries attest to
her suffering more powerfully than verbal complaints. By exposing her
wounds, Mrs. Oka signals she is not ashamed that she defies her husband.

—Stan Yogi, "Rebels and Heroines: Subversive Narratives in the Stories of Wakako
   Yamauchi and Hisaye Yamamoto," *Reading the Literatures of Asian America*, ed. Shirley Geok-lin
   Lim and Amy Ling (Philadelphia: Temple University Press, 1992), 131–33

VELINA HASU HOUSTON

12-1-A is about the Japanese American World War II incarceration experience and focuses on the uprooted Tanaka family, who is assigned to a camp in Poston, Arizona (where Yamauchi herself was interned). The Tanakas and the other Japanese American detainees in the camp are trapped in what easily could be termed a political nightmare, especially if one is an American citizen with certain inalienable rights. They do not know how long they will be there. Indeed, they do not know if they will ever leave the dismal camp alive. The hysteria of the media, the American government, and the American people has stripped them of their citizenship and dignity, and they are living in fear of very uncertain, undefined, perhaps nonexistent futures. The storm blows in Yo to the Tanakas' tiny quarters. Yo is alone because her father was sent to another detention camp. Her manner, her politics, and her fortitude send different messages to each of the Tanakas about what two short weeks in a prison camp can do to a Japanese American. Yo is one of the strong female presences in the play. On the surface, she is cynical and manages to laugh at the utter impossibilities of her existence. When she talks about the barrack for single women in which she lives, she says the women are lined up on narrow beds like inmates in a prison and Mitch Tanaka, a young Nisei, laughs at her, saying it is what she gets for being a woman. With bitter humor, Yo agrees: "Yeah, for being a woman. For being single. For being Japanese. I think someone up there dealt a stacked deck." The wind also blows in two young Nisei, Ken Ichioka and Harry Yamane. They all wonder how long the war will go on and how it will affect their lives. Mrs. Tanaka, mother of Mitch and Koko, is told that the outcome of the war will determine their fates, but as Yo points out, there will be no liberation for Japanese Americans. "In a war, Obasan, one country wins; the other loses. . . . We all look the same to them. We lose both ways." Mrs. Tanaka's concern is amplified by the senselessness of unlawful imprisonment and the fear of death. Yo counsels her not to worry: "What is there to fear? Life? Death? Just roll with the punches."

The survival of the women in the camp is of particular interest. The politics of their lives are in turmoil. The older generation represented by Mrs. Tanaka was learning to be American and trying to acculturate the children. Then the U.S. government put them in camps, and the ideals, customs, and behavior of the country seemed ludicrous in the face of such destructive racism. Yo survives her political and personal losses by hiding behind a tough exterior. Still, Yo remains the optimist. When Koko wonders if she will ever have the kind of love Yo once had, Yo hopes the best for her, and we glimpse the sentiment underneath the cynicism. Koko, on the other hand, is a teenager who feels the world has disappeared. She cannot afford to have hope, nor can she afford to bend to convention and leap into the routine of life in the camps. She was a bud in bloom, nipped in mid-furl. She may be fated to live out her life in this stage of aborted womanhood, looking for answers with the utter, quiet belief that there simply are none for a Japanese American woman in the United States. Koko can never treat the camp world as normal and firmly believes that normalcy is a thing of the past, left to the ignorant, obedient, or complacent. She holds on to this belief to keep her dreams alive. Like Emiko in *And the Soul Shall Dance*, she must keep her soul dancing even if her exterior self is emptying bed pans and experiencing a longing [for Ken], which she cannot confess to its catalyst. While all this emotion takes its toll, there is a visual symbol: a guard tower that slowly encroaches upon the environs of the play, looming larger and larger and representing a sense of the characters' realization of their plight, which leads to politicization, challenges, and political imprisonment. How Koko matures through the course of the play and how political actions—those of the U.S. government incarcerating citizens and those of the no-no boys (who answered no to two questions on the camp questionnaire referring to service in the U.S. Army and renunciation of loyalties to Japan)—affect her life and that of her family are apparent in the touching conclusion to this play that explores the politics of the Japanese American incarceration without sacrificing the personal.

   —Velina Hasu Houston, "Wakako Yamauchi," *The Politics of Life: Four Plays by Asian American Women*, ed. and with commentaries by Velina Hasu Houston (Philadelphia: Temple University Press, 1993), 39–40

GARRETT HONGO

In the late story "Ōtŏkŏ," a retrospective piece in her grand style, Yamauchi reveals that part of her technique has sprung not only from stylistic roots in contemporary letters, but has had to do with her feeling for an extraordinary tradition—that of Japanese *song*—both the *shigin* tradition of narrative balladry and the one of folkloric and popular love songs. She has, as a background to her method and as a sort of emotional pitch-point, perhaps attached her new, American stories to the wealth of emotions invoked by Japanese lyricism. In "Ōtŏkŏ," as she has done previously in "And the Soul Shall Dance," Yamauchi quotes lyrics and invokes pentatonic, Oriental melodies from popular prewar Japanese culture and the older folk traditions of Japan, importing a wealth of memories and associated emotions, invoking the past and a separate inheritance of aestheticized melancholy unavailable in literature written exclusively in English. There are in these invocations a special, almost religious quality of emotion and an evocation to its lyric cadences quite unlike anything I know of in American letters. These are closer to the melancholy of Appalachian gospel tunes and have the resolute quality of black spirituals. When Yamauchi calls them forth, I feel, deep in my bones and in the strange, nearly imperceptible rushing of my blood, that huge inner evacuation of alienation and mystery that is a signal of the abolished emotional dissonance and historical distance between myself and those Issei immigrants who might have been my own ancestors.

In "Ōtōkō" two aging Nisei siblings, a brother and a sister, chilled by contemporary suburban life, spend the occasion of the summer solstice together. The brother brings a recording of old Japanese songs that remind them of the distant life they began with, raised by Issei parents homesick for Japan. As Yamauchi dubs fragments of the Japanese lyrics into her story, as she invokes the melodies that accompany them, the brother and sister reminisce, fade back into similar memories, and draw together. My reader's heart lifts, even three generations removed, to the invocation of these songs and Yamauchi's juxtaposed stories of travail about those who spoke a language very different from the English I live in now. The Japanese term *sabi* is a word for the indescribable, plangent sadness for the poverty of being itself. It is a mode that invokes pity and a cast of mind in which compassion is born, and it is Yamauchi's grand mode as a writer. The storytelling and the narrator's voice themselves become pitched to the extraordinarily melancholy and balladic emotional tone of the Japanese tunes, and Yamauchi's writing seems to gain in susceptibility to the most delicate and ephemeral of recollections—whole swaths of generational experience. She describes Issei farmworkers inhabiting a transient hotel:

> Sometimes in the evening they would play wistful Japanese melodies on harmonicas or wooden flutes . . .
>
> The older men were scruffy and bowed from years of scraping along on their knees picking strawberries . . . and from bending over low grapevines. Their pants were caked with mud. They shook them out at night over the balcony. Conversations were colored with sexual references, and they laughed lewdly at the jokes. They spent their leisure playing *hana* (cards) or drinking sake which my mother kept warm for them at ten cents a cup.
>
> Once a man staggered off to the courtyard and passed out on the dirt, the ocean breeze cooling him, the sun warming him like the fruit he'd spent his youth harvesting. In the late afternoon he woke and walked away brushing himself off, without shame, as though it were his natural right as a man. Fruit of the land. (240)

The aesthetic enables her own nearly rapturous connection with the things of the earth and the small details of living, and, empowered by a rich tradition of stylized melancholy invoked by song, Yamauchi's stories, even as they describe an outer world, become symbolically invested with the amazing ability to reproduce the complicated and otherwise somewhat silenced *emotional* character, the Rilkean "inner life," of Nisei and Issei experiences.

—Garrett Hongo, "Introduction," *Songs My Mother Taught Me: Stories, Plays, and Memoir,* by Wakako Yamauchi (New York: The Feminist Press, 1994), 9–10

VALERIE MATSUMOTO

Art occupies a special place in the hearts of Yamauchi's women and men ⟨in her collection *Songs My Mother Taught Me: Stories, Plays, and Memoir*⟩. For an Issei couple in "And the Soul Shall Dance," the scratchy records of Japanese songs played on a Victrola provide a nostalgic connection to their homeland. "They take me back home," the husband realizes. "The only way I can get there. In my mind." For the Nisei teenager Aki, the violin music of a newly hired farm-hand expresses her awakening sensuality and yearning for love.

The desire to create art is often stymied. On one level, the Japanese American artist must grapple like all other artists with the challenge of conveying a personal vision: "How does one paint love, a swelling of the heart, flowing of glands? How does one paint an unshed tear, a joy?" asks the protagonist of "The Coward." "Can a color, a shape bring to mind all the recollections of childhood, or terrors or tendernesses yet to know?" On another level, this Nisei woman artist faces obstacles particular to her gender and ethnicity: she finds herself caught in the conflict between pursuing the life of an artist—as exemplified by that of a European man she has met at museums—and remaining faithful to her upbringing and sense of responsibility. On the verge of an adulterous affair, she balks. "We're hurting no one," her artistic mentor reassures her. "My life is to feel." "But I live a more prosaic life," she replies. "I couldn't do this to people I love." She ponders wryly,

> Yes, prosaic. That was my heritage and my mother's before me and
> countless daughters of mothers before her. Yes, commonplace.
> Ordinary. Was his perhaps the real way to live: love and give totally,
> without regret or obligation, to extend one's self to the limit of his
> capacity of love, of pain, of feeling, of giving and taking, and still be
> true (darling in my fashion) to the commitments one's made? (145)

Their very languages distance them. His lacks vocabulary essential to hers: commitments, compassion, love, anguish.

Commitments, compassion, love and anguish form distinguishing thematic threads throughout Wakako Yamauchi's stories and plays; glibness and false glamour have no place here. As Valerie Miner writes in her afterword, "Selfishly, I wish these pieces had been collected long ago, when I was a younger writer, because they offer nourishment and momentum. Yamauchi's passion for truth—at the expense of sentimentality and dogma—gives me permission, no, requires me, to tell the truth in my own work."

Reading these stories transports me to the sand dunes, creosote bush and searing sun of my childhood in the Imperial Valley. In strong, clear language that reflects the austere beauty of the desert, Yamauchi portrays complex, timeless conflicts of love battling obligation, youthful ambitions chafing against parental worldviews and the struggle to realize dreams in a hostile environment. Her skillful exploration of the relations between immigrants and their American-born children makes visible the tensions and delicate negotiations between generations, as well as the shared roots that bind them.

—Valerie Matsumoto, "Migrant Writer," *The Women's Review of Books* 12, no. 3 (December 1994): 9

PATRICIA HARUSAME LEEBOVE

⟨Wakako Yamauchi's *Songs My Mother Taught Me*⟩ investigates the rippling effect of poverty during the American Depression and the era's rampant racism. At a recent reading of her work, Yamauchi said that her goal was to write "the perfect story." She hoped to write stories that would make "the hearts of her readers bleed." It is this confrontation with despair and ultimate resolution that give this collection its power.

Many of the Japanese Americans that Yamauchi creates have internment camp histories. This collection of short stories and plays, edited by Garrett Hongo (who arranged them according to "Country Stories," "City Stories," and "Recollections"), spans the continuum of identity that exists within Japanese-American culture: first-generation immigrants, photo brides, Nisei (second generation), and Issei (third generation). The story "Shirley Temple Hot Cha-Cha" is a painful exploration of a young Kibei couple (children of Japanese Americans who are sent to Japan to be educated because of the limited opportunity in the United States during the 1930s and 1940s) and who later are trapped by poverty in wartime Japan. By the time they finally return to America, they have lost family members and have missed the opportunities both countries once had to offer them. "The Handkerchief" breaks the taboo among Japanese-Americans of a mother making the impossible choice between sacrifice for the sake of her family and the survival of the self. The story is told from the perspective of the mother's middle son, who expresses the feelings of resentment and abandonment of an entire culture that expects a woman never to act to satisfy her own desire. "In Heaven and Earth" explores the difficulties and emotional desolation of a widow left farming a desert landscape while trying to raise her children, particularly her daughter, during the Depression. This story was rewritten by Yamauchi and produced by the New

York Public Theater as a play titled "The Music Lesson." What remains unspoken makes the story so effective. Yamauchi's timing is impeccable and her insinuations powerful enough to allow the reader time to catch up.

> —Patricia Harusame Leebove, "Memories: Writing into the Future," *Belles Lettres* 10, no. 2 (Spring 1995): 66

B I B L I O G R A P H Y

Books

Songs My Mother Taught Me: Stories, Plays, and Memoir (ed. Garrett Hongo). 1994.

Plays

And the Soul Shall Dance. 1974.
Shirley Temple, Hotcha-Cha. 1978.
The Music Lesson. 1980.
12-1-A. 1982.
Songs That Made the Hit Parade. 1985.
The Memento. 1986.
The Trip. 1988.
The Chairman's Wife. 1990.
Not a Through Street. 1990.